FINDING YOUR WAY
THROUGH FIELD WORK

 SOCIAL WORK IN THE NEW CENTURY

Richard K. Caputo, *Policy Analysis for Social Workers*

Michael Reisch, *Social Policy and Social Justice*

Lisa E. Cox, Carolyn Tice, and Dennis D. Long, *Introduction to Social Work: An Advocacy-Based Profession*

Mary C. Ruffolo, Brian E. Perron, and Elizabeth Harbeck Voshel, *Direct Social Work Practice*

Urania E. Glassman, *Finding Your Way Through Field Work*

SOCIAL WORK IN THE NEW CENTURY

FINDING YOUR WAY THROUGH FIELD WORK

A Social Work Student's Guide

URANIA E. GLASSMAN
Yeshiva University

Los Angeles | London | New Delhi
Singapore | Washington DC

Los Angeles | London | New Delhi
Singapore | Washington DC

FOR INFORMATION:

SAGE Publications, Inc.
2455 Teller Road
Thousand Oaks, California 91320
E-mail: order@sagepub.com

SAGE Publications Ltd.
1 Oliver's Yard
55 City Road
London, EC1Y 1SP
United Kingdom

SAGE Publications India Pvt. Ltd.
B 1/I 1 Mohan Cooperative Industrial Area
Mathura Road, New Delhi 110 044
India

SAGE Publications Asia-Pacific Pte. Ltd.
3 Church Street
#10–04 Samsung Hub
Singapore 049483

Publisher: Kassie Graves
Editorial Assistant: Carrie Montoya
Production Editor: Kelly DeRosa
Copy Editor: Megan Markanich
Typesetter: Hurix Systems Pvt. Ltd.
Proofreader: Rae-Ann Goodwin
Indexer: Rick Hurd
Cover Designer: Gail Buschman
Marketing Manager: Shari Countryman

Printed in the United States of America

Library of Congress Cataloging-in-Publication Data

Glassman, Urania, author.

Finding your way through social work : a social work student's guide / Urania E. Glassman.

pages cm. — (Social work in the new century)

ISBN 978-1-4833-5325-8 (pbk.)

1. Social work education. 2. Social service—Fieldwork. 3. Social service—Practice. I. Title.

HV11.G56 2016
361.3071'55—dc23   2015023617

This book is printed on acid-free paper.

15 16 17 18 19 10 9 8 7 6 5 4 3 2 1

Brief Contents

Detailed Contents

Case Illustrations

Foreword

As the editor of the SAGE series, Social Work in the New Century, I am delighted to introduce this latest book that focuses on social work's "signature pedagogy," field education. The series' goal is to provide students, faculty, and social work professionals with the theoretical foundation, conceptual tools, knowledge, skills, and ethical principles required for effective practice in today's rapidly changing local, national, and global context. Written with wisdom, insight, and humor by Ronnie Glassman, a leading social work educator, this volume provides expert guidance for undergraduate and graduate students to help them navigate the entire field work process and its many potential pitfalls.

Although field education is widely proclaimed as the most critical component of a social work student's training and the development of the profession's core practice competencies, it frequently presents the most difficult challenges for students. While many students are well prepared for their academic coursework, they are often less able to handle the complex and ambiguous practice situations with which they are confronted at their internships. Students are placed in circumstances that are outside their previous life and work experiences and are required to work with people whose values, goals, lifestyles, and daily problems are far different from their own. To become effective practitioners, students are compelled to examine their underlying assumptions, resolve tricky ethical dilemmas, learn how to apply broad theories to a specific context, negotiate complicated organizational and community environments, and grapple with what it means to be a professional. Recent demographic changes, increased socioeconomic inequality, and the fiscal impact of policy developments on field agencies have further complicated this complex educational landscape.

In her book, Dr. Glassman skillfully guides students through this landscape. She is sensitive to the issues students—particularly beginning students—face and to the multiple relationships that all students must develop to have a successful field placement experience. Through well-placed, pithy vignettes and case examples, she illustrates how many common student mistakes can be avoided and how inevitable missteps can be corrected. Glassman also distinguishes the specific issues faced by BSW, first-year MSW, and advanced MSW students as well as those that affect students who use their place of employment as an internship. She analyzes the roles of key players in the field education process (field instructor, task supervisor, faculty field liaison) and presents invaluable advice to students on how to maximize the educational opportunities their field agencies provide.

Michael Reisch, PhD, MSW
Daniel Thursz Distinguished Professor of Social Justice
University of Maryland
School of Social Work

Preface

This text is presented to reduce students' stress and anxiety as you approach field work in the first and second years of the MSW program, and in senior year of the BSW program. Created from the perspective of a long-standing field director, it aims to achieve smoother field work experiences for student readers. The text gives practical approaches to students for succeeding in field work. It takes students through routes that bypass or navigate the typical obstacles they will meet. By escorting a student through the maze that is field work, the author maximizes a student's ability to learn in field work.

Field directors seek to groom students by highlighting favorable and undesirable actions and setting them on the path for maximizing the learning experience in field work. This text provides a field director's insight about students' successful and adverse approaches to field work. Its many real-life case illustrations and vignettes shed light on your role as student and the roles of those involved with you in field work. The goal is to prevent the numerous mishaps that occur down the road, which may lead to disruptions in field work or even failures.

Yet this is not a how-to book simply because field work is not prescriptive. The book briefly describes experiential learning models for field work. It includes how to use supervision and coaching from a field instructor. It affirms your development of artistry in using yourself to perform the social worker role rather than to just read about it in a book.

The book is organized in four major parts with several chapters in each.

Part I: Understanding Where You Are Heading, describes the student's direction. It includes an overview chapter on field work, a chapter on experiential learning in field work, and one on social work competencies that students will have to attain, with strategies for coping with your many concerns. Case illustrations further highlight coping.

Part II: The Design and Structure of Field Work explains the structure and framework of field work. Chapters discuss ways of getting your relationships with clients started, how to best forge a productive relationship with your field instructor, facing your discomfort about being vulnerable or judged, and how to access insight and direction from your faculty field advisors. Interactions with field instructors and clients are found in many case illustrations.

Part III: Transforming the Desire to Help into Professional Competence: From Caring to Learning How to Do shows how students enact professional skill. Included are chapters on how students acquire and apply social work competencies in the foundation senior year of the BSW program and first year of the MSW program. The attainment of competencies in the advanced second year of the MSW program is presented. Case illustrations of process recordings, in which competencies and practice behaviors are labeled, are used to provide clarity about practice, and to demonstrate the field instruction process.

Part IV: I Feel Like Spaghetti—All Strung Out presents chapters dealing with the feelings and challenges students encounter in the intricate relationships that have to be sustained with clients, field instructors, and faculty advisors. Strategies for dealing with the many conflicting demands of family and friends are presented, along with ways of managing the effects of personal history on your field work. Added focus is provided for students in moving on to the next stage—whether it is heading to a job or further education. Included are many case illustrations.

The case illustration method in this book represents a unique field work learning tool that brings students' accomplishments and dilemmas to light, thereby igniting your understanding and catalyzing learning.

Students look forward to field work with eagerness and expectation. With the passing of time, social workers have asserted that field work was the most memorable experience of their social work education. It is my hope that this book will influence your effectiveness with clients and stimulate the achievement of your fullest potential in field work.

Acknowledgments

The path of my career has always seemed to be propelled by the good advice and fabrications of friends and colleagues. This project is one more opportune happening.

My sincere gratitude goes to SAGE—to Kassie Graves, associate director and publisher, and Dr. Michael Reisch, Social Work Series editor, for enticing me to craft a field work book for students. Kassie has never failed me in her unwavering support of this and my earlier work. Michael's stalwart commitment to and understanding of my approach to this text has been heartening.

I also must acknowledge Leah Mori for so capably copyediting the knots and Megan Markanich for her meticulous review.

What fun—sharing my views directly with students. My indebtedness to them can never be fully rewarded. I hope I have paid tribute to their lives, their need to earn a living, or just the fact of the limited life experience of their youth.

The field educators' network, especially the New York Area Directors of Field Instruction and NANFED (North American Network of Field Educators and Directors) are all part of the village that emboldens me and stimulates the scholarship in field education. I thank them for this.

The late field directors, Dr. Helene Fishbein and Dean Schneck, and educator, Dr. Catherine Papell, were grand visionaries and prime movers whose legacy sustained my work.

My gratitude to Dr. Charles Garvin for his generosity is infinite. Bart Grossman, Jane Hassinger, Len Kates, Ellen Sue Mesbur, Marvin Parnes, Virginia Cook Robbins, and Louise Skolnik have been significant partners in my work.

I am privileged with the collegiality and friendship of my coworkers. The ensemble at Wurzweiler School of Social Work at Yeshiva University is unrivaled. I am particularly grateful to my talented field department team: Raesa Kaiteris, a field work genius with students and field instructors who has been with me unconditionally for well over a decade; my support Gloria Marin; and to the recent members who have graciously and ably assisted me in the tumult of the work—Jill Becker Feigeles, Frances Montas, and Heleena Van Raan. I could not have asked for a better cohort to be proud of every day.

My thanks go to Nancy Beckerman, Joan Beder, and Michele Sarracco for expertly steering students and agency staff through many field work intricacies. Charles Auerbach, Jade Docherty, Lynn Levy, Susan Mason, Jay Sweifach, and Wendy Zeitlin have always given me their unqualified help. It is quite a boost that our dean Carmen Ortiz Hendricks is a field work author and former field director; I deeply appreciate and value her staunch support. Agency field educators Heide Rosner, Rebecca Szmulewicz, and Karen Zuckerman have contributed greatly to my reflections for this volume.

Valued friendships with Erika Sanchez, Gloria Scorse, and Pat Strasberg have been central to my life.

My life partner and husband, Ron, and our sons, Dan and Alex, have lovingly endured the endless time frame of field work. Ron is a captivating teacher and prolific writer about democracy, equality, and social institutions. Dan, an astute economic and social observer, uses his research skills as a financial analyst and journalist. Alex, a philosopher theologian, employs his social work insight to write about the concept of a person. They are magnetic and draw people to them. I am extraordinarily proud of them. They contribute to my social construction of reality as I try to reflect upon what I do through their unique lenses.

The extended family includes my bighearted niece Nancy Glassman Pasqual and her David and Noah, the Florida Glassmans, the Kyriakopoulos and Alatza units in Greece and in America, and the rest of the Kalamata cohort. By their side is the will of my parents, Denis and Magda Ernest (aka Anastasopoulos). All chronicle strength of character, a social ethos, and love of learning that is part of our shared heritage.

I, along with SAGE, gratefully acknowledge the contributions of the following reviewers:

Patti Aldredge, *Virginia Commonwealth University*
Terrence T. Allen, *North Carolina Central University*
Jane E. Barden, *Valparaiso University*
Jennifer L. K. Boiler, *Rutgers University*
Pamela Brodlieb, *Long Island University Post*
Patricia Carl-Stannard, *Sacred Heart University*
Nicole M. Cavanagh, *University of South Carolina*
Bronwyn Cross-Denny, *Sacred Heart University*

Sandra K. Edge-Boyd, *University of Oklahoma*
Staci J. Jensen-Hart, *Idaho State University*
Rachelle Kammer, *Fordham University*
Mark Lamar, *Rutgers University*
Katherine Perone, *Western Illinois University*
Don Schweitzer, *Pacific University*
Janet Tyler, *Cairn University*
Mindy R. Wertheimer, *Georgia State University*

This book is dedicated to the students who undertake the challenge of social work because they have the insight to envision a rewarding future.

About the Author

Dr. Urania E. Glassman's role as director of field instruction spans 30 years. Her social work specializations are field education, group work, and clinical practice. She is currently principal investigator of a $1.4 million grant from the U.S. Department of Health and Human Services Health Resources and Services Administration (HRSA) for Wurzweiler School of Social Work (WSSW), Yeshiva University, to train second-year students in clinical field placements with high-risk adolescents and transitional age youth. Her recent volume with SAGE, *Group Work: A Humanistic and Skills Building Approach* (2nd ed.), provides underpinning for the training design. Dr. Glassman maintains a long-standing clinical practice with individuals, families, and groups.

She has written and presented papers on field education processes and experiential learning, training field educators, group work, and clinical practice. Dr. Glassman served on the Council on Social Work Education (CSWE) Commission on Educational Policy during the time when social work competencies were defined and field education as social work's signature pedagogy was branded. She was instrumental in the development of the CSWE field education symposium (now the field education track) and of the NYC Red Apple Chapter of the International Association of Social Work with Groups as well as cofounder of NANFED (North American Network of Field Educators and Directors) and has served as chair of these initiatives.

SAGE was founded in 1965 by Sara Miller McCune to support the dissemination of usable knowledge by publishing innovative and high-quality research and teaching content. Today, we publish more than 850 journals, including those of more than 300 learned societies, more than 800 new books per year, and a growing range of library products including archives, data, case studies, reports, and video. SAGE remains majority-owned by our founder, and after Sara's lifetime will become owned by a charitable trust that secures our continued independence.

Los Angeles | London | New Delhi | Singapore | Washington DC

Part I

Understanding Where You Are Heading

Chapter 1

Introduction to Field Work: Experiential Education

INTRODUCTION

This text is designed to set you on the right path toward beginning field work at all levels—first-year and second-year master in social work (MSW) field work and senior-year bachelor in social work (BSW) field work. Written from a field director's vantage point, it provides a practical and theoretical framework for achieving success in field work. You will find counsel; suggestions; options; and, at times, humorous reflections to guide your thinking and the stance you would like to take as you approach field work. Some items are geared to senior-year BSW and first-year MSW students, while others are specific to second-year MSW students. There are some details you need to know and likely some adjustments to be made in your thinking in order to maximize your field work experience. So if you're ready, read on.

As a student in field work, you will practice with people. You will develop professional relationships with your clients who need something from you and it is up to you to figure out what they need. These relationships should have depth rather than superficiality. This depth comes from a clear understanding of the theories and professional values highlighted in class that provide the foundation to help you recognize clients' needs and issues. To be clear, field education is not only about learning theory and quoting from the text. Something more is required. Field education is about practicing—using knowledge and values to guide your work. Therefore, you will apply the theory that you've learned in your coursework to live situations with clients.

DEVELOPING COMPETENCY IN FIELD WORK

Experiential learning theories inform social work field education. Dewey's (1938/1963) educational principles focused on the relationship between knowing and doing. Building on those principles, Kolb (1984) developed a model of student learning styles, while Schon (1984) emphasized reflective practice in professional education (Schon, 1990). Goldstein (1993) focused on field education itself. More recently, Shulman (2005) and others (Gardner & Shulman, 2005) examined signature pedagogies in the education of various professionals.

To further guide your field work experience, the following approaches of experiential education will be used throughout this text to help you reflect on your development of social work competency in field work.

The Feedback Loop

The feedback loop (Bogo & Vayda, 1998) illustrates the learning process in the supervisory interaction between a field instructor and student that highlights the development of reflective practice (Schon, 1984). You will experience this process frequently. Step 1 represents the student's practice with a client—whether an individual, family, group, or community. Step 2 is the student's reflection and observation of the client. Step 3 involves connecting theory to a student's actions and reflections, which occurs during the meeting between field instructor and student. In Step 4, a professional response is developed with the field instructor for the student to use in future meetings with the client (Bogo & Vayda, 1998). This new client interaction begins Step 1 in the feedback loop again. This process is demonstrated in Figure 1.1.

The Field Instructor as "Coach"

The concept of the teacher as "coach" (Schon, 1990) highlights the training you will receive while completing your field work. This resembles the feedback

Figure 1.1   Feedback Loop

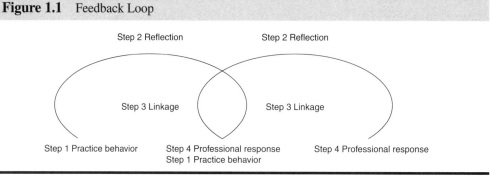

Source: The Practice of Field Instruction in Social Work: Theory and Process, 2nd edition, by Marion Bogo and Elaine Vayda. © University of Toronto Press 1998. Reprinted with permission of the publisher.

a hitting coach gives to a baseball team member upon observing him or her at bat or how a piano teacher prompts a piano student's performance. The field instructor listens to the student, absorbs details from process recordings about interaction with clients, and uses understanding of the student's intentions to provide feedback.

A field instructor as coach is meant to support you and guide you even in the most difficult times. For instance, one such supervisor's strengths are described as (1) her unfailing responses to her students and staff in the moment; (2) that she always has a useful, action-oriented response to their crisis with a client; and (3) without fail, she finds a way to pick them up and sustain their morale. She is heralded by all staff but generally not known beyond the confines of the hospital (Anonymous, personal communication, 2012).

Stages of Experiential Learning

In her classic work, Reynolds (1948) identified five stages of experiential learning. You will experience these stages in your field work and beyond. Stage 1: Acute Self-Consciousness represents the anxious feelings of starting field work. Stage 2: Sink or Swim describes taking the plunge and diving into the work. Stage 3: Knowing What You Have to Do But Not Always Being Able to Do It shows the student's progress toward competence. This stage continues throughout a student's schooling. Stage 4: Mastery and Stage 5: Being Able to Teach will occur after a student's social work program is completed.

The Johari Window

The Johari Window (Luft & Ingham, 1955) is a visual framework from small group theory. When applied to field work, it clarifies how learning about yourself occurs with feedback from others. The four quadrants in the Johari Window show how feedback an individual receives expands knowledge about him or herself. The four quadrants of self-knowledge are as follows:

- Quadrant I: Issues about myself that are known to me and known to others—open area
- Quadrant II: Issues about myself that are known to me and unknown to others—hidden area
- Quadrant III: Issues about myself that are unknown to me and known to others—blind area
- Quadrant IV: Issues about myself that are unknown to me and unknown to others—unknown

These are represented in Figure 1.2.

Figure 1.2   Johari Window

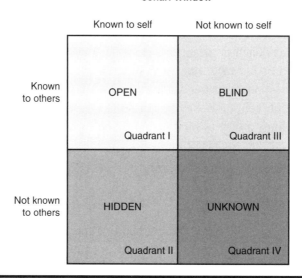

Source: Luft, Joseph (1999). The Johari Window: A Graphic Model of Awareness in Interpersonal Relations. In Cooke, Alfred L., Brazzel, M., Saunders Craig, A., and Greig, B., (Ed.), *The Reading Book for Human Relations Training, 8th Edition* (pp. 51–54). Silver Spring, MD: NTL Institute for Applied Behavioral Science.

Figure 1.3   Johari Window—How Feedback Expands the Public Area

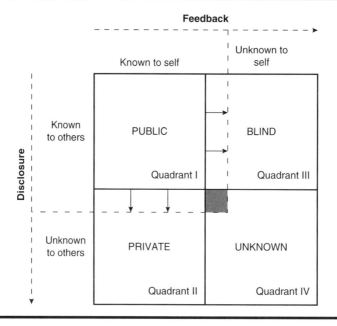

In the feedback loop process in field instruction, students expose their work, the hidden area in Quadrant II, and their field instructor provides feedback in Quadrant III, the blind area. The purpose of feedback is to increase the size of Quadrant I—the open area of issues known to self and known to others. Thus, the issues in Quadrants II and III become exposed and shared. This is depicted in Figure 1.3.

The exchange of disclosure deepens communication between you and your field instructor, which, in turn, deepens your role with clients. Extensive discussion on the process of field instruction will be found in Chapter 5.

HOW TO MAXIMIZE EXPERIENTIAL LEARNING IN THE FIELD

This text examines frustrations and potential obstacles in working with clients and developing practice skills. It provides tools and supports to help you address and deal with these issues. Several helpful maxims are introduced to help you make the most out of learning in the field and will be discussed in detail in future chapters.

Know Thyself

The first maxim is to "know thyself." The Greek philosophers usually attribute "Gnothi seauton," know thyself, to Socrates (Delphi, 7th century BCE). In practicing with clients, you will have to understand how their issues and needs impact you. You must also recognize any personal feelings of uncertainty and awkwardness.

It is important to know who you are in the learning process. In constructing a desk from IKEA, some people start assembling immediately, reading the instructions as they go along. Others review the instructions thoroughly before undertaking the task (Kolb, 1984). The person who jumps in will find the thorough reader to be frustrating. Some students will read chapters about schizophrenia before seeing the client; others will conduct more research after meeting the client. How you approach learning provides you with further self-awareness. The popular model of Kolb (1984) describing four typologies of learning styles has more recently been expanded by others (Honey & Mumford, 2006).

Embrace Being a Learner

The second maxim is to embrace being a learner. This involves accepting that you do not know everything and suspending your need to prove that you do. It means giving yourself to the experience and allowing yourself to be supervised. With this comes accepting the labels of "student" and "intern." You are undertaking an internship, not a job.

Start Where the Client Is

The third maxim is to start where the client is. You will hear this daily. Your challenge will be deciphering where that may be. Your classroom and field instruction will help you apply the necessary critical thinking to determine where the client is. The point is that you must make every effort to start with your client's agenda, not your own.

Accept the Ambiguity and Feelings of Uncertainty of Social Work Practice

The fourth maxim is to accept the ambiguity and feelings of uncertainty of social work practice. This asks you to give up your expectations of prescriptiveness and the need for hard-and-fast rules. Rather, you must be able to go where the client takes you—at least some of the time. Facing the unknown of first meetings will challenge you as a beginning practitioner. Try not to avoid these feelings.

Do Not Skip Over Preparatory Empathy

The fifth maxim is to not skip over preparatory empathy. Following the dual aspects of preparatory empathy boosts your connection with your client. First, review the literature about this type of client. Second, reflect upon how you would feel in that client's shoes. These tasks have no shortcuts. Consider how you would feel if you were a 37-year-old who, in college, had your first psychiatric hospitalization. You were diagnosed with schizophrenia and now you still cannot work where you had wanted—in nursing. Use this reflection by preparing yourself to be acutely attuned to the client's needs when you meet.

Integrate Social Work Theory and Values Into Your Work With Clients

The sixth maxim is the ethical imperative to integrate social work theory and values into your work with clients. As a professional learning experience rather than a job, field education requires you to effectively apply knowledge and values to the client situation. Professional ethics dictate that you rely on theory and values to direct your work.

Embrace Artistry as Your Individuality in Professional Use of Self

The seventh maxim is to embrace artistry as your individuality in professional use of self. Becoming an effective social work practitioner requires that you embrace your creativity. Picasso didn't just paint any old woman. He painted one whose eyes, limbs, and torso were viewed from different angles. You, too, need to do this, although you are not yet Picasso. Use of self is how you uniquely approach a client situation through the lens of professional theory and values. However, at this point you will not have complete creative control—your ideas should be tested out with your field instructor and your classmates, all of whom are part of your Johari Window.

By harnessing your self-reflections, keeping up with readings, and writing process recordings, you may even form a creative approach for helping your clients.

CASE ILLUSTRATION 1.1

FORMULATING CREATIVE USE OF SELF IN A CRISIS SESSION

Deborah, a 24-year-old first-year student, has been concerned about her 89-year-old client, Morty. She anticipated that the flooding in his Brooklyn community from Hurricane Sandy probably created a visual that reminded him of the devastation in his town in Russia during World War II (WWII).

At their first meeting, he talked about the displacement of the Jewish population in his former Russian community and his new life here. He is one of many Russian Jewish residents in the area who came to New York City decades earlier after the former Soviet Union allowed the Jewish population to leave. Deborah has some understanding of WWII and the Russian role in defeating Germany. Being Jewish, she also knows about his community.

Deborah's agency has a program to help Hurricane Sandy survivors. She knew Morty had been evacuated and was located at an assisted living site. Although Deborah did not suffer storm damage, many of her friends did. She expected Morty to be out of sorts. However, when she visited him, he was happy to see her and said that he was so impressed with how quickly the Americans distributed food and relocated everyone. This would never have happened elsewhere. Deborah was amazed, and although she had prepared to talk with him about his "plight," she saw that was not his experience. Instead, he talked about how liberating it felt to leave Russia.

Deborah was uplifted by his attitude, thinking that he handled the storm better than her friends. Gaining new perspective, she told him that she was inspired by the way he handles difficulties and that even the war experiences he had do not seem to have unnerved him now. He hinted that there is much he does not like to talk about and prefers the positive and reiterated how impressive the community had been.

(Continued)

(Continued)

Meeting with the Field Instructor

Deborah and her field instructor discussed how she can find out more about Morty's life, including allowing him to share some negative experiences. Her field instructor credited Deborah for shifting her focus from an expected plight into being where the client is and hearing his reaction to the hurricane relief efforts. Her life lesson from Morty has Deborah thinking about how to share his positive attitude with her fellow students. In this situation, Deborah embraced artistry by using her own knowledge of history to show her client she understood his story and his history. Deborah and her field instructor decided she should tell her practice class about Morty's impact on her. Although Deborah has much more to learn about how to explore negative feelings, her connection to the client fostered her artistry in her use of self—even as a beginner.

Discussion

Deborah's artistry in her use of self is evident. She used the two parts of preparatory empathy before seeing Morty. She knew the history and is in touch with her own feelings. In dealing with the unexpected, she moved to where the client is. She then reflected on her feelings and the impact Morty has on her.

FRAMEWORK OF THIS TEXT

This book is constructed in sections with several chapters contained in each section.

Part I: Understanding Where You Are Heading provides an overview of field education. The social work competency framework for foundation year and the second year of field work is provided.

Part II: The Design and Structure of Field Work contains concrete tools for a successful entry into an agency and a viable beginning. This part provides discussions of the relationships you will develop with your field instructor and your faculty field advisor.

Part III: Transforming the Desire to Help Into Professional Competence—From Caring to Learning How to Do details practice dilemmas in the student–client relationship and the development of competencies throughout the foundation year and advanced second year of field placement. In these chapters, you will come to see why work with clients seems easy when you read about it in a book yet can be so difficult in your practice reality.

Part IV: I Feel Like Spaghetti—All Strung Out is centered on the stressors and stressful relationships you will encounter in all spheres that will impact the professional role. These may be with clients, field instructors, and faculty. Discussion about countertransference and how to manage your own personal history is included. Other stressful relationships that will impact your role in field work are considered, including the personal relationships and demands of family, friends, and significant others. These added factors, which focus on transitions, endings and moving forward, are discussed.

SUMMARY

This chapter is the first step in your journey to a successful field work experience. As you have seen, field education is about practicing and utilizing theory and values to guide your work. Equally important is self-reflection. Utilizing the approaches discussed in this text, such as the feedback loop, allowing your field instructor to play the role of coach, the five stages of experiential learning, and the Johari Window, will help you to grow in your role as a social worker. Finally, it is important to remember that you will experience frustrations and obstacles in your work with clients. Keep the seven maxims in mind to help you connect to your clients and adapt to various situations.

Chapter 2 describes the social work professional role in field work.

Everyone associated with this volume wishes you every success as you begin. We hope the tools supplied here will guide your positive and productive performance.

Student Qualities and the Transformational Process

INTRODUCTION

Most students enter social work programs primarily out of a desire "to do good," "to help," "to change things," and "to make a difference." This want usually comes from something personal that is known to the student but is not widely known to everyone else. Some students may have acted on this desire by volunteering or interning. For other students already employed in human service positions helping clients, enrollment in a bachelor in social work (BSW) or master in social work (MSW) program is seen as the next step in professional advancement and skills development. Students who are changing careers have concluded that making a difference as a social worker will provide a more rewarding professional life.

ELEMENTS THAT STUDENTS BRING TO FIELD WORK

There are a number of elements that students of all experience levels bring to field work. This section will explore the elements that newer students will likely have, as well as those that more experienced students will have. Case illustrations will help to demonstrate these points.

New Students—Foundation First-Year MSW Students and Senior-Year BSW Students

New students bring three elements to a social work program that frame their entry into field work.

1. The first element is the vital personal factor that explains the student's drive to join the profession; this may or may not be known to others at the start.

2. The second element is comprised of the approaches and potential difficulties the student encounters in the transformational process of field education. This is usually below the surface and may be unknown even to the student.

3. The third element is made up of the catalysts and barriers to learning and developing social work skills. It is also found below the surface and may be unknown to the student.

Coming to terms with the known and hidden factors you will bring to the learning process in the field can facilitate a wholehearted engagement in the experience. You will see this in the next two case illustrations.

CASE ILLUSTRATION 2.1

TRANSITIONING FROM ANOTHER CAREER

Eric is a 35-year-old with a previous well-paying job selling pharmaceuticals. Upon concluding that he was involved in creating an unnecessary need for drugs and because of his own psychotherapy, he decided to enroll in a social work program. While he will openly share that working in business allowed him to save the funds to make a career change, he won't readily disclose his negative feelings about the pharmaceutical industry. Due to his prior experience, he requested a field placement in psychiatry. Since psychiatry is not available to first-year students, he was placed in a children's residential treatment program.

Eric has prepared to grapple with how psychotropic medications are being used with children in treatment. These concerns were not shared with the field office. He decided that immersion in the field placement will further his knowledge of the interface between psychopharmacology and clinical practice and what he views as ethical dilemmas. Eric wants to help these vulnerable children most of all and has committed to the placement.

CASE ILLUSTRATION 2.2

TRANSITIONING FROM A SUBSTANCE ABUSE COUNSELOR JOB

Annabelle, a 43-year-old BSW senior, has a similar issue on the use of drugs. She is a recovering addict who held a job as a substance abuse counselor in a drug-free treatment setting. She has negative feelings about harm reduction programs and believes the drug companies have been marketing methadone maintenance (MM) programs as an alternative treatment. She comes to social work school to learn more about how to help clients become substance free.

Annabelle's placement will be at an agency with an MM treatment program. She will have individual clients and two women's groups that focus on specific issues of violent relationships and children in foster care. She was told that several group members will be drawn from the MM treatment program. She informed the field office that she does not want the placement since she does not believe in the "harm reduction" treatment model.

Discussion

Both Eric and Annabelle have similar beliefs about the use of psychopharmacology. Eric appeared to be more willing to suspend judgment and work within the practice model of his placement. Annabelle seemed less able to suspend judgment. One wonders if she will be able to work within the boundaries of that site. Whether or not the entry-level student knows enough to challenge existing practice is not the issue; instead, trying to understand why this approach is used is within the domain of the student role. Annabelle has made a cautious decision to accept the placement.

Both students need to bring their concerns to field instruction. While neither student may transfer clients or undermine the treatment plan, both may bring the issue to practice class to allow collective feedback to inform them. The classroom's experimental domain has a high tolerance for viewing a range of options, whereas field work is highly regulated because real clients are involved.

Your school decides where to place you, even when you believe you should be placed at a particular site because you have experience with that problem or know the population. This is shown in three case illustrations.

CASE ILLUSTRATION 2.3

FIRST-YEAR STUDENT WANTS A PLACEMENT IN DOMESTIC VIOLENCE

A 28-year-old first-year student, Harriet, had great difficulty exiting an abusive relationship. She came to social work school to learn how to help women in her own ethnic community who are "devalued" and who face domestic abuse.

Discussion

If you are this student, you must remain open-minded to the various settings where skills to enhance client empowerment may be developed. At this time, you are not qualified for a domestic violence setting because you lack the coursework in family dynamics and therapeutic techniques. Additionally, prior field work does not indicate that you are prepared to address and deal with your own reactions to women's situations that will be too similar to your own.

Simply put, what you want to handle may be too complex at this time. You, too, will have to disengage the emotion out of the disappointment so that you may go forward and learn.

CASE ILLUSTRATION 2.4

FIRST-YEAR STUDENT WANTS TO ADVOCATE FOR LGBTQ COMMUNITY

A 25-year-old gay man, Nick, is committed to working as an advocate for the lesbian, gay, bisexual, transgender, queer (LGBTQ) community, with a special interest in a mental health placement. Although it is a second-year placement, he believes being gay credentials him for the placement.

Discussion

Nick will have to alter his route. This is a common issue for all students: Although your background informs your understanding, it does not credential you as a social worker. Credentials come from learning, and a mental health field placement requires several prerequisite courses.

Nick might explore the generational factors in the LGBTQ community instead. The gay man he is now in his 20s is not the same 20-something gay man from

1975 who is now over 60. His history of mental health treatment vastly differs from Nick's. A field placement with senior citizens could offer Nick potentially enriching client histories and a chance to work with gay seniors. Locating a gay-friendly nursing home for placement could be eye opening, as would other endless venues. A middle school placement working with children on their learning issues, while also doing group work focused on friendships, bullying, and the future, could provide a rich field opportunity.

CASE ILLUSTRATION 2.5

FIRST-YEAR STUDENT DOES NOT WANT A FIELD PLACEMENT IN THE LGBTQ COMMUNITY

A 30-year-old gay man, Ted, came to school because social workers are the people he has counted on as his counselors and supports since his childhood diagnosis of HIV. He feels he can put himself in the social worker chair. He did not ask to work with gays or in HIV. He disclosed his positive status to the field director and asked for a different environment with different issues. He was happy to be given a placement in a senior center, and he loves it.

Discussion

In Nick's and Ted's examples, the personal self—that is, being gay—does not define who they will be as a professional. Their needs are as different as their life circumstances. It may be that Ted has to be far away from his experiences in order not to be defined by them. Nick does not need as much distance from his own situation to be of help. Harriet's personal self, being a domestic violence survivor, may define her for the time being. However, it does not sufficiently prepare her to be in a domestic violence placement at this time. The highly sensitive disclosures to the field director provide helpful data to guide the field placement process.

More Experienced Students—Second-Year MSW Students

While personal circumstances and individual motivation may be similar, the second-year student who has already completed a foundation year is better prepared to control personal factors effectively in field work than a beginning first-year MSW or senior-year BSW student. This contrast can be seen in the next case illustrations.

CASE ILLUSTRATION 2.6

SECOND-YEAR STUDENT DEALING WITH A FAMILY ILLNESS AND LOSS

Betty, a 38-year-old second-year student, lost her 7-year-old daughter to cancer eight years ago. She enrolled in social work school because she received support from social workers throughout her daughter's illness and in hospice. She hopes to use her firsthand knowledge of parental grief and parenting sick children to help others.

For second-year field work, she requested an oncology site and was interviewed by the adult unit social work supervisors. After two intensive interviews where Betty's self-awareness and grief issues were probed, the social workers concluded that she has sufficiently dealt with her daughter's death and will lend much to their medical setting; she was accepted as an intern.

CASE ILLUSTRATION 2.7

FIRST-YEAR STUDENT DEALING WITH A FAMILY ILLNESS

A 24-year-old first-year student, Vera, asked to meet with the educational coordinator at an agency working with sick children. On first look, she appeared to be a good candidate due to camping and tutoring experiences with children. Further exploration by the agency educational coordinator revealed that she was not suitable for that setting because her father is currently battling cancer. That information had not been provided in her meeting with field work faculty.

Vera expressed disappointment in a follow-up discussion with a field faculty member. She had not considered that some work with clients may pose difficulties because it hits too close to home. It is important for Vera to disengage from the disappointment. It is a common belief held by beginning students that having firsthand knowledge of an experience equips them to help someone in a similar situation. However, many do not know that when their own life issues surface during their work with clients, these may interfere with the effort and the client will not receive optimal service.

Discussion

Betty's prior personal history was ready to be put to good use in the interest of clients. In Vera's case, this could not take place. By not bringing her father's illness to the attention of field office faculty, the first-year student showed that she had not recognized the potential impact her own situation might have on her work with clients. Even if Vera had disclosed her situation, the placement with sick children would have been too risky for her. No evidence was available to the school that she had accumulated the skill to handle the impact of personal factors that would occur in her role with sick clients. On the other hand, Betty had a track record from first-year field work. While Vera was coping with a difficult personal issue in the present, Betty's situation was well in the past.

Betty and Vera may not bring up their personal issue in class, nor will these special issues define their role as students in field work. However, Betty will purposefully consider the countertransference aspects of the work. Vera will be more apt to raise the issue by chance, not by purpose.

In the end, the point for your understanding is this: *Accept that you are not yet prepared to handle some of the issues that you want to handle.* That's fine. No one is going to hold that against you. That is how it goes in all professional learning.

TRANSFORMATION IN FIELD WORK

In field work, you will find it necessary to spend time in self-reflection. You will have to evaluate your personal ideals or goals, potential barriers to your growth, and ways to hone your skills. This is all a part of the transformative process of field work.

The Personal Element That Brought the Student to the Program

Although the student may know the personal ideals and goals that have brought him or her to social work, these reasons may be unknown to the agency and to the field education office. Wanting to use psychotherapy techniques instead of psychopharmacology or wanting to help women in violent relationships are examples of such initial personal goals.

Consider what your personal goal may be and how it defines your desire for field placement. As you move through the learning experience, your personal goal will be transformed into professional skills. Your initial goal may be altered or even abandoned. For example, Harriet may conclude that daily exposure to domestic violence situations may be too conflict laden to be pursued upon graduation. Or Nick may find himself eager to develop programs for senior citizens with HIV.

Potential Difficulties in the Transformational Process

Many potential difficulties related to the transformational process of field work are often unknown to the student. For example, the beginning student does not immediately realize that having a father battling cancer will interfere with a field placement related to sick children. However, educators tend to know about these issues. When in this predicament, it is important to your professional growth to accept feedback from the field office staff that you are not ready for this placement. Being insistent with the field office is not a productive strategy. Suspending judgments, redirecting your thinking, and focusing on the fact that field education is not primarily about you is more effective. The student–agency match is about the clients and what the student can do to help them.

Potential Barriers and Catalysts to Learning and Developing Skills

It is necessary to recognize that you are immersed in a transformational process that includes openness to how practice is undertaken at your agency. This stance will positively impact your learning situation in field work. Participating in the transformational process involves appreciating the need for social work values to prevail even if they conflict with your own. A student may disagree with the treatment methods being used, then overreact and search the literature to support his or her fixed opinion rather than to fact find. This is a barrier to developing skills. Rather, the student's role is to gather knowledge; learn about many practice approaches; understand the research; and factor in social work values rather than to be guided primarily by feelings, biases, and opinions.

This encompasses knowing that professional skills and treatment models supersede personal opinions about how to practice. This may involve performing tasks that you did not think you would perform and using skills you may not have ever anticipated you would own.

FIVE ELEMENTS OF FIELD WORK

In order to do better than just survive in your field work, it is necessary to begin with some understanding of the elements of social work field education that include (1) agency mission, (2) student's assignment, (3) field instruction, (4) embracing the role of student, and (5) time frame requirement.

Agency Mission

Before and upon your arrival, you must learn about your agency's mission and program. This includes their scope of practice, community context, and social institutional context. Know their funding and their organizational structure. Know the names of staff in your immediate program and familiarize yourself with the names of others, the various programs, and locations of other sites.

Learn about the context of the agency's community: its demographics; socioeconomics of residents; ethnic, religious, and racial breakdowns; and any specific unique historical or current factors. Know if there are key employers in the area, as well as lost employment due to business closings. You may be placed in a Native American community with a history of conflict with those living on the reservation. Your senior center may be in a predominately Dominican neighborhood yet its members represent the Jewish and Puerto Rican groups that formerly lived in the area.

Funding influences are major, and at least half of you will experience a funding-related upheaval at your agency requiring adaptation. Governments and nongovernmental groups, philanthropies, and religious institutions will fund most agency programs.

Student's Assignment

Your agency and field instructor are prepared to assign tasks to enhance the development of your professional skills and competencies and meet the school's curriculum. A second-year MSW assignment will reflect your concentration or specialization. If you specialize in group work, half of your weekly direct practice time at the agency should be working with three groups, while the rest of your time can be with clients and families. If you specialize in child welfare practice, then your clients in the middle school should consist primarily of children in foster care or in a prevention program and their families.

A first-year student or a senior-year BSW student will have a broad assignment in a context that allows the development of practice skills with individuals, families, groups, organizations, and communities. The extent of each assignment will depend upon the agency. A home care agency will undoubtedly give you individual clients and their families. A group assignment will have to be created later. In contrast, a student in a community center may have one after-school children's group and two senior citizen groups. Individual clients should emerge for short-term counseling and entitlement referral as crisis issues arise. A community assignment may involve working with seniors to prepare the center's online newsletter.

As tasks are developed and identified, students and field instructors should consider the goals that each assignment is designed to meet.

Field Instruction

The field instruction process has a structure and rhythm that you will follow in order to be successful and to benefit from the experience. The field instruction process begins with the scheduling of regular weekly meetings. While there will always be chances to make informal contact with your field instructor, the bulk of learning revolves around the more formal field instruction conference. For this meeting, you will come prepared with an agenda, questions, process recordings, and a note-taking device. Being coached requires your proactive involvement in presenting what you do to your field instructor for review.

Your preparation of process recordings and other written documents to be reviewed by your field instructor provides further structure and support and enhances the necessary processes of the feedback loop. Your learning occurs if you are proactive.

To receive coaching, you must be open and willing to suspend prior judgments and conceptions. This includes being accepting of what you are told even though you do not believe you have been given enough evidence. It is often the case that what you consider lack of evidence is you not yet knowing enough. Accept and learn to live with the ambiguities. You are there to learn, and that involves doing and following instructions.

For example, imagine you went to your voting center to vote and the police officer told you to wait in line before you could enter. You waited. You might ask why. A few minutes later, you see officers emerge with a handcuffed person in tow. The point is, you would not have known why you had been told to wait outside. Nor would that information be immediately given to you. Then, two weeks later you might find out that the handcuffed person was part of a sting operation. As a social work student, it may take you longer than two weeks to figure out why you were told to do something in a certain way. Thus, you will have to do what you are asked and maintain decorum with regard to what you do not know.

Say that your field instructor makes the point that when you start a group, you should ask them what they hope to get out of the group. He tells you not to engage each person in a long presentation of their reason for being there but to focus on identifying several of the common themes. You are puzzled and say that you prefer asking each person to present his or her own special issue in a go-around. Your field instructor says not to do that and asks you to read Chapters 4 and 5 on group formation. You are being coached. Your batting stance is not right, and you will go into a batting slump. By contrast, the gains you will reap from accepting the coaching and then reading Chapters 4 and 5 will be far greater.

Embracing the Role of Student

The prior issue leads directly to this one. You have been competent somewhere else, and now you want to feel and to show that you are competent here. This is hard. One student owned a jewelry business; one was a day trader. Gabe is a substance abuse counselor; Myra is a parent of eight. While in prison for armed robbery, Freddy finished college. Whatever you had been doing, you left it to pursue social work. Eventually, your maturity and prior skills will show and be recognized in what you are doing.

Or, it might be that upon graduation from college you moved back into your parents' house to attend the MSW program. Now at home the autonomy you found in college is gone and upon going to field work you feel the same loss of autonomy. You were once a college peer counselor; you supervised camp counselors, but now you are supervising no one and you have to answer to many.

Students are expected to participate in very particular social behaviors. In other words, social work students are expected to behave in a certain way. A medical intern does not undertake a surgical procedure without knowing what it is and how to do it and without having received direction from a teaching doctor. Similarly, a social work intern must do what is required to learn the social work role, and the requirements become more apparent once a student is engaged in the learning process. Therefore, as a student, when you start a social work group you ask the members what they hope to get out of the group. Accessing each member's deeper issues will come later. First, you work on engaging all. While this may feel counterintuitive, once you see it in action, you will understand its meaning.

Within the relationship with your field instructors, you have a part to play in inviting your field instructor to coach you. You do this by putting yourself in the student role and demonstrating openness to feedback and the learning experience. (Further details about field instruction will be found in Chapter 5.)

Time Frame Requirement

Accreditation standards (Council on Social Work Education [CSWE], 2015) mandate the number of hours that students must complete in their field work and the types of face-to-face assignments they should have within that time frame. The minimum number of field work hours required of MSW students during the two-year period is 900 hours—450 for first-year field work and senior-year BSW field work and 450 hours for second-year field work. Schools develop calendars to meet educational and agency needs. Many MSW and BSW programs require more than the minimum number of hours during a typical academic year to ensure the student's integration into the agency, to provide for depth in the client assignment, and to foster opportunity for competency attainment.

SUMMARY

This chapter has described the elements that students bring to their social work programs, which can play a role in how they conduct themselves during field work. It is important to disclose all known elements to your field instructor so you can be placed accordingly and gain the most growth and help the most people with your experience. Self-reflection and transformation are a part of this process, and you will grow in the three major components of social work competencies: (1) performing the social work role, (2) using knowledge to inform practice, and (3) applying professional values in performing the role. In addition, there are five components of social work field education that will help you thrive in your field work: (1) knowing your agency's mission, (2) reaching goals in your assignment, (3) understanding the field instruction process, (4) embracing the role of student, and (5) fulfilling the time frame requirement for field work.

Chapter 3 describes what students have to do when approaching their entry to field placement agencies.

Chapter 3

Securing Agency Acceptance

INTRODUCTION

When you think about introducing yourself to your new agency, you may feel anxious and fearful, and although you want to help people, your insecurity and lack of experience may surface and you will question your ability to help. On the other hand, you may feel that with your background or experience, you should be able to help—after all, you had another career, volunteered at a senior center, or had a college internship at a psychiatric center.

While your experience contributes to the agency's view of you, it is not most important. A student's background is only one part of his or her acceptance at an agency and may be of secondary importance. More vital to an agency is that you represent your school and that the school has vetted you in the admissions process. The agency expects that you will meet classroom requirements and proactively engage in field instruction. Moreover, the expectation is that you will reflect on the emotional unrest you may face as a result of working with clients. Being a trustworthy student is the agency's expectation. Having to carry malpractice insurance highlights the seriousness of your role. The agency has to know you are there wholeheartedly and that any preemptive decision to disqualify this placement because of your limited knowledge has been put to rest.

Do not be discouraged that your various skills may not be important. They will be—but not as you envisioned them and not yet. For now, what matters most is that you enter the system as a student, knowing that your place is to take direction, to listen, and to meet the agency's expectations.

This chapter highlights aspects related to entry into an agency.

AGENCY ENDORSEMENT OF STUDENT AS WORKER
WITH CLIENTS

Professional social work with clients has unimaginable complexities that reach far beyond your desire to help. Agencies are mandated by a range of government, corporate, and licensing processes to provide services in particular domains, such as targeted populations with needs to be met or social problems and psychosocial dilemmas to be addressed. These defining parameters are called "scope of practice." Funding and licensing determine what an agency may and may not do. Social workers and other related professionals usually provide services within an agency and its mandate.

An agency's educational function occurs when professionals in that setting wish to train the next generation. For some agencies, the service function and educational function have evolved jointly, similar to that of a teaching hospital. Learning how to teach social work will deepen agency staff members' understanding, while also establishing their relationship with a school. The invitation to beginning interns carries with it the hope that they will provide additional service while giving the staff a chance to serve as mentors.

In order to trust an intern with their clients, agency staff must be confident that the student intern will work openly with good will and without reservation to establish the field instruction relationship. They have to be confident that the intern will diligently utilize classroom knowledge to inform his or her role at the agency and with clients. The student must work to sustain the agency's confidence. The student recognizes social work's ethical requirements and strives to meet these in practice and at school. Students are expected to possess self-awareness and maturity to respond professionally and deal accordingly with emotions that come from client interactions. Note again that the seriousness of these baseline requirements is reflected through the mandate that all students carry malpractice insurance. This is purchased through the school.

PREPARING FOR INITIAL AGENCY MEETING

There are a number of things to do to prepare for your first meeting with a potential agency. These include preparing a résumé, completing a field planning form, scheduling your meeting with the agency, evaluating your social media presence, and choosing the right attire for your meeting.

Résumé

Some agencies and schools will require a student to submit a résumé in addition to a field placement form for entry to a field placement. When students apply for field placement at an agency, their role is not that of employee. They are not expected to know and carry out the range of social work tasks at the site. However, they are expected to meet client needs.

Agency field educators are curious about students' backgrounds. Agency staff would like to know if students have worked in previous fields and what those fields were. If students are recent college graduates, agency staff want to know about the focus of their undergraduate learning. While agency personnel consider these experiences, they are not most important.

More essential to the agency is the student's ability to communicate profession-ally. Thus, your first item of communication will be either a résumé or a form you submitted to the field office. Use the school's template to write it and have a faculty member review it so that anything unsuitable will be returned to you to be redone. All communication should be professional and succinct, with special attention to grammar and spelling. To put it clearly, there is no room for misspellings and grammatical mistakes on a résumé.

In each year of your studentship, the résumé should be revised to reflect your current and future career in social work. If you are a second-year student, your first-year field placement or senior-year and junior-year bachelor in social work (BSW) placements should be listed under educational experience and intern-ships. These should not be listed under work experience. Undergraduate and other graduate education is listed first. Field placement should be listed below education. Then employment is identified, and after that in a separate category, volunteer experiences are added. See Figure 3.1 for an example of a résumé.

Field Placement Form

The school's field office will ask you to complete a field placement form, which includes identifying information and learning goals. Schools often send this infor-mation to your agency. Do not gloss over this. Prepare an intelligent form, with enough information in it to present yourself as an open learner willing to work with a range of populations and in varied problem areas.

Provide a brief overview of your undergraduate education, including major and honors, and your work and volunteer experiences. The following are sample questions on a placement form:

1. Describe your learning goals for first-year field work.
2. List your social work–related job experience.
3. List your social work–related volunteer experience.
4. List in reverse chronological order current and prior employment.
5. Are there geographic and other constraints related to field work we should know about (e.g., religious observance, time constraints, transportation restrictions)?

(See Appendix B for a typical format.)

Figure 3.1 Résumé of Quiche Lorraine

RÉSUMÉ

Quiche Lorraine
1422 Boulevard St. Michele
Paris, France
(342) 290-xxxx   quiche.lorraine@xxx.fr

EDUCATION

Paris School of Social Work   Master in Social Work May 2016
Paris, France

London School of Economics   Bachelor of Arts 2012
Major: Philosophy, Magna Cum Laude

FIELD PLACEMENTS

Second Year—Specialization in Clinical Social Work   September 2015–May 2016
Institute for Psychosocial Therapy
Lyon, France

- Individual counseling of clients with schizophrenia, bipolar disorder, and other diagnoses
- Group work—conducted activities therapy group, creative writing group, and women's group with patients in day treatment program
- Crisis Mobile Unit—ACT team member
    Conducted outreach and crisis intervention with team to provide medication for patients, monitor their well-being, and prevent rehospitalization
- Received individual supervision from licensed social worker weekly
- Prepared and submitted weekly process recordings for supervisory review

First Year—Generic Social Work   September 2014–May 2015
Odeon Community Center
453 Boulevard St. Germaine
Paris, France

- Worked with immigrant mothers of children in early intervention program. Populations were primarily from African and Middle Eastern countries. Met weekly in group. Saw individual mothers.
- Focus on children's French language development skills to prepare them for school
- Worked with education staff in teaching parenting skills and child development for mothers
- Facilitated adolescent group of girls to focus on issues related to school, culture conflict with parents, and friendship and other relationships

EMPLOYMENT

French Language Teacher   September 2012–May 2014
Manchester High School
Manchester, UK

- Teach beginning and advanced French classes
    o to ethnically diverse high school students
- Create innovative program inviting native French speakers to classroom
- Develop anti-bullying program and curriculum for the school

Camp Counselor and Unit Head   Summers 2009–2012
Orchard Street YMCA Settlement Camp
New York, NY, USA

- Theater director for French language production

VOLUNTEER EXPERIENCE   September 2010–2012
Intergeneration Projects
Seniors and High school students
Manchester, UK

Introductory Communications

You are likely to be asked to e-mail a résumé or write an e-mail to an educational coordinator or field instructor to arrange a meeting. A cover letter or e-mail cover letter is needed when forwarding an attached document or requesting an appointment. This should express interest in the agency and willingness to meet at their convenience, without obstacles. Be certain of your spelling. *Spell check is not enough.* It will not catch *there, their, they're,* or *led* and *lead.* The following examples speak for themselves.

CASE ILLUSTRATION 3.1

GLENN'S INFORMAL E-MAIL TO THE DIRECTOR OF SOCIAL WORK AT A CHILDREN'S RESIDENCE

"Hey Diane, it's me, Glenn. i hope we can talk about my filed placement Soon. . . . do u want me to call you? You can text me at 888–444–1234"

CASE ILLUSTRATION 3.2

GLENN'S FORMAL, PROFESSIONAL E-MAIL TO THE SAME DIRECTOR

Dear Ms. Stewart,

I am writing to you because Dr. Finley, director of field work at my school, Rodeo University, let me know that you might have a field placement opportunity available in the children's residence at Kids, Inc. I am a first-year student, and I look forward to the possibility of being placed in your agency.

I am available to meet with you at your convenience.

Thank you for your consideration.

Sincerely,
Glenn Rollins
First-Year Student, Rodeo University
glennrollins@student.rodeo.edu
888–444–1234

Social Media Review

Next is another domain requiring your attention: your social media. Scrutinize your Facebook page. Begin by asking yourself if you would want a client or future employer to see your Facebook in its current form. Remove some of the overly personal material, including masquerade party costumes that are known to be among the worst offenders. Delete the party pictures with beer kegs. Whether or not you will be placed in alcohol and substance abuse treatment is not the issue. Some clients may have these issues. This is a good opportunity to prepare a more sophisticated self-presentation. Soon-to-be clients will sneak a peek, not to mention agency staff. Almost everyone is looking for a little bit of gossip. It should not be about you.

Scheduling the Agency Meeting

To make a positive impression at a prospective agency, you should be perceived as a student who is eager and enthusiastic about the site, mature, responsible, literate, well spoken, and professional, with an open mind about people—all types of people.

Before making a phone call, it is important to have all relevant information readily available, such as the name and title of the person you are calling. Address the person as Mr., Ms., Dr., or by any other relevant greeting—not by first name. Students have likely been involved in professional relationships with college professors, employers, and physicians. Usually, addressing them on a first-name basis was the result of relationships that developed. At the outset, it is safest to err on the side of professional formality. In some settings, social work staff will routinely go to court and bring the student along. The judge is addressed as "Your honor," and the social worker as well as the intern as "Mr." or "Ms."

CASE ILLUSTRATION 3.3

INITIAL PHONE CALL

"Hello, this is Glenn Rollins. I would like to speak with Ms. Carina. I am a student from Rodeo University and was referred by my school to speak with her. Is she available? May I leave a message?"

"Who at your school referred you?"

"It was Dr. Madison, director of field work."

"Oh, you are calling about an internship. Ms. Carina is not available right now, but she will want to speak with you. May I have your number, please?"

Leaving your name and number will suffice. If your call was not answered, your voice mail message should be brief. In this case, you left a voice mail message, and Ms. Carina must return your call.

CASE ILLUSTRATION 3.4

FOLLOW-UP: THE RETURN CALL

Ms. Carina returned your call and had to leave a message. However, your cell phone has a lengthy musical greeting that kept her on the line longer than she desired. Delete the music. Replace it with a simple greeting. This will become your professional number for messages from your school and agency, as well as future employers. Purge the voice mail greeting that says, "If you have something good to tell me, leave a message. If you do not, tell it to my girlfriend; she will use her discretion in telling me or not."

Discussion

When you are at last able to speak to Ms. Carina, do not ask her too many questions about the agency or the neighborhood. It is more effective to visit the agency website to learn about their services and figure out how to get there yourself. When you are on the phone, expressing interest, making the appointment, and accommodating to the days and times presented are important. It is not a good idea to say, "I am not sure I want to work in developmental disabilities." Climb out of what is familiar or comfortable to you and be open.

Attire, Appearance, Presentation

Having settled the voice mail and telephone issue, you must now consider what you have to do to get through the door. First, there is your attire. Women should wear a blazer, pants, skirt, or a suit. Men also need a blazer with a shirt and tie. Jeans should not be worn even if the setting is informal. The jewelry should be low-key for women and men. Sneakers and flip-flops are not appropriate. Most hospitals prohibit all sandals because exposed feet are at risk in settings with a great deal of movement and commotion. Women should be sure that lingerie straps are not visible. Men and women must be mindful of clothing that is suggestive or formfitting. In work with clients, everything matters. Simplicity and maturity in style matter. Someone working at home for the past 10 years, who is used to a casual style, probably needs to invest in a business wardrobe suitable for the professional world.

An attorney, accountant, or journalist constructs an outfit to gain the respect of clients. The student's deliberate approach to attire shows clients they are important and that the student believes the professional role is important.

If the agency is near the mall, shopping bags and other irrelevant materials should not be brought to the interview, nor should large backpacks. A briefcase and a notepad will suffice. Phones should be silenced and put away. Water bottles and coffee cups should not be brought to an appointment.

Briefcases and handbags belong on the floor, not on the interviewer's desk. If you find yourself at a conference table, the same applies. Conference tables are meant for note taking and hold only meeting-related items. Water and coffee cups are permissible when offered to participants.

What students actually wear to field work each day will be determined by the setting. Some settings are casual; others are formal. You will find that out quickly.

THE INITIAL AGENCY MEETING

Whether you are a first-year master in social work (MSW) student, BSW student, or a second-year MSW student with more experience, you must prepare for your initial agency meeting and, once there, handle yourself professionally and respect- fully. However, the focus of your meeting will differ with your experience, as you will see in the following sections.

First-Year MSW and BSW Students

Before your meeting, reflect upon what you have been doing in recent years. If you have been a student, think about what you have learned and are learning. Consider the extent to which your job and volunteer experiences are applicable to the agency. Looking through the agency website to learn about their programs, the agency community, and the issues dealt with is helpful. Reading about the target population provides understanding. For example, if this is a shelter for homeless families, considering the uncertainties and shame faced by a high school student who is homeless and living there deepens perspective.

Saying to an interviewer, "I have no experience," does not help your cause. It indicates that you did not consider the clients served or did not look deeper into the situation. This statement puts the responsibility for the student's learning on others,

CASE ILLUSTRATION 3.5

STUDENT RESCHEDULES APPOINTMENT WITH AGENCY STAFF

A first-year student, Victoria, made an appointment with Doreen, a field instructor at a Head Start program. Three days later, she canceled it and rescheduled for the following Tuesday at 10:00 a.m. She called on the way to say the subways were delayed and arrived 45 minutes late. Doreen felt very inconvenienced because she had arranged for several staff to be present. After the meeting was rescheduled, she again arranged for staff to be present. Then Victoria was late and staff had other tasks.

Doreen tried to determine if Victoria has empathy for the needs of parents and knowledge of child development. Victoria was vague and then said that she could not come to placement in the early morning because she has a morning job. Since this placement needs a student in the morning, Doreen ended the meeting, saying that this placement will not be feasible for Victoria.

The field instructor phoned the field director to report that Victoria could not arrange to be available in the morning. Doreen also reported that Victoria canceled the initial appointment and came late to the second one. She stated that she was not impressed with the student who seemed disorganized, scattered, and not focused on the meeting. The field director was surprised about Victoria's job and said she would hold a meeting with her to review all of these issues. She apologized for wasting the agency's time.

not on the student. On the other hand, doing homework before the interview primes the student to say, "I saw a little bit of what you do here on your website and I hope to have a chance to learn how to contribute in some way."

It is imperative that you present yourself professionally and are prepared for your meeting. This next case illustration demonstrates what can happen if you are not.

Second-Year MSW Students

Before meeting with an agency social worker, considering your experience with previous clients is excellent preparation. Delineating the clients' issues and your role in working with them on these issues gives you useful material. Prepare to talk about certain assessments you made of your clients, what issues were hard for you to work with, and what you learned in that process. Reflect upon your own self-awareness and countertransference issues. Talk about your successes and failures with clients. Share about the group work and community social work you did. The following case illustration demonstrates what can happen if you do not prepare for an interview.

CASE ILLUSTRATION 3.6

SECOND-YEAR STUDENT LACKING PREPARATION

A second-year student, Moira, did not prepare for her interview at a medical center. She consequently stumbled over discussing her work in her senior-year BSW nursing home placement. She missed the similarities between the settings and the potential carryover to this medical placement of skills learned in senior year. Mr. Hastings, the educational coordinator, informed her that she would be discharging stroke and heart bypass patients to rehabilitation programs. At the nursing home, she worked with the short-term patients in the rehab unit. Yet she didn't discuss the connection between the two settings and the work she would be doing. The educational coordinator found her to be passive and disengaged. He later called the field director to say Moira was unsuitable and ill prepared for a medical placement.

Moira could have received a great deal of praise for showing her strengths at the meeting if she had done some focused and thoughtful preparation ahead of time.

One caution: Do not say, "I did not learn anything in senior year or first year." That's not possible. It is best to think about what you are about to say. This comment devalues your own learning and the agency and school you were or are in.

Also, never speak badly of your prior field placement, agency, field instructor, your school, or anyone at your school. Never! These types of statements indicate that you may not be thoughtful or trustworthy. If there was a problem at your placement in the previous year, seek assistance from the field director on how to discuss these issues.

If you are being interviewed at a mental health setting and you are unfamiliar with the *Diagnostic and Statistical Manual of Mental Disorders* (either the *DSM–IV* [2000] or *DSM–5* [2013]), peruse it beforehand and enroll in a course that provides the supporting knowledge to start your second year. Have a plan in mind for what you will share about your own psychotherapy. Social work staff want to know about your guided self-reflective experiences as it relates to your learning in the field work setting. If your new placement is in substance abuse treatment, prepare how to discuss your own history if you have one. You should be aware that if you are in recovery you will not be permitted to disclose this part of your history. Most agencies are clear that you are not to share your personal histories with clients.

Perhaps at a new placement a student will be asked to run support groups for refugees and immigrants. Before meeting at the agency, a crash course on world history and geography should be taken. Learning which countries agency clients are coming from, where these are on the map, and the conflicts and economic and health issues people are facing in those countries is necessary preparation. Clients may be from the former Soviet Union. Does the student know why it is referred to as the "former Soviet Union"? The student also must exhibit some understanding that while Spanish is a client's native language, the Dominican Republic is neither like Argentina nor Colombia, and Puerto Ricans have U.S. passports.

QUALITIES THAT AGENCIES ARE LOOKING FOR

You made it through the interviews and will be starting at the agency. Put all your beliefs and views on the back burner. Forget your prior skills for the time being. Here you will find further information about what agency staff want from you, first and foremost. These details will give you direction, before any part of your knowledge, background, and prior skill can become useful.

Trustworthiness

To be seen by others at the agency as trustworthy, the student has to present himself or herself as a person who is open to the agency, to the staff, and everything that occurs there. Students must indicate in their presentation of self that they understand staff have expertise that they do not have and that they value what they are doing. A student who believes otherwise must stop and redirect because his or her assumptions will be incorrect. Students will not possess the expertise of agency staff; thus, they need to be open to learning from staff so they can help clients. You can begin by tuning in to your biases—any beliefs that you have because of something you learned or where you worked. Reflect on what you bring from jobs or internships about counseling or case management or from giving advice to many people.

Understanding and demonstrating recognition that agency staff have expertise that the student lacks makes the student trustworthy. Consequently, the agency and its clients are not put at risk by you following your own ideas, as opposed to doing something you are told to do. A student must be guided by the dictum "do no harm to clients." Included is the necessity to keep up with classroom learning and to maintain grades of B or better, which are required in social work programs. These are the qualities that make a student trustworthy.

CASE ILLUSTRATION 3.7

STUDENT'S INTERVIEW AT A MIDDLE SCHOOL

Kyle had been a case manager in a program for young adults with developmental disabilities. In his interview at a middle school support program for youngsters with learning issues, he described the work at his previous job. The field instructor discussed the agency's intense work with parents. Kyle admitted that he had done minimal work with parents at his job because it was not encouraged since the agency's focus was on clients' independence. The interviewer asked him how he would feel meeting with parents. He said that at his job at times parents were seen as overprotective. He went on to say that he realizes these are younger children who need parental involvement. He said that he welcomes a chance to work with parents in the middle school and at the same time get to know the children. His first case is with the mother of an 11-year-old with several learning issues.

Discussion

Kyle showed flexibility in his approach to the population and depth in his response. He showed willingness to practice with parents and the middle school population and demonstrated his knowledge of the older clients' learning issues. These behaviors indicated trustworthiness with agency clients. This openness gave the field instructor the impetus to assign a parent to Kyle.

Humility

Humility follows right after trustworthiness. If you are humble then you are able to accept your own lack of expertise, your newness in the situation, and your role as a student. Embracing your role as student is essential. This can be demonstrated by showing curiosity when confused about a statement or procedures at the agency. If a social worker or staff member makes a statement about a procedure or service approach at the agency, before jumping in to ask a question or challenge the policy, the student needs to pause and reflect. Avoid saying, "This is not how I was taught to do this." It is best for you to sit with the confusion for now.

You may ask why. The answer is simple: No matter how much or how little you know, you will find much of it to be confusing at the start. This is because your agency's actions are being done through a professional lens you have yet to learn about. Therefore, do your part by assuming your role as a student to digest. Time for questions will come once you have done more reading and reflecting. You will be able to ask intelligent questions that have grown out of your ability to integrate what you are being told with what you are learning in the classroom and in your relationship with clients.

Reliability

Reliability involves predictability. A predictable student can be counted on and is considered a dependable intern—one who the agency believes will follow through. Reliability in an internship, simply put, consists of several key rules students will have to follow.

Sticking to Your Schedule

Your schedule has been worked out with the school, your agency, and with your input. You are essential, and you are being counted on to be at the agency at your designated day and time.

Being on Time ALL THE TIME

It should go without saying, but students have to be where they are expected when it comes to clients—all the time without fail, *on time.*

Submitting Paper Work on Time

It is expected that progress notes on client meetings, assessments, intakes, and all papers are well produced and in a timely manner. Progress notes are part of professional accountability. Agencies do not receive reimbursement for work in the same way that physicians are not paid until they submit their patients' medical forms. Thus, students will continually work on establishing professional reliability throughout the entire internship.

Keeping Appointments

Students have to keep appointments. Therefore, if you have been casual in your personal life or overly spontaneous about social engagements, including casually making and breaking engagements, this behavior is not allowable professionally. This is not meant to take away your personal spontaneity. It is meant to put you on the path and help you avoid difficulties because casualness does not work professionally.

Let us start with the initial appointment you make to visit the agency. Once it has been made, the appointment should not be changed. Appointments are serious and require serious intentions. This is the first step in establishing credibility as a reliable professional.

Along with the first meeting at the agency, appointments that are made in the professional domain should not be changed. Careful examination of one's calendar *before* setting an appointment with a client, another professional, community member, or with anyone in the agency is required. Keeping an organized calendar is vital. Once an appointment is put on a person's schedule, the rest of his or her time has been planned to accommodate that meeting. Others may have been included in the meeting. Your cancellation creates inconvenience for everyone. Your name is on their calendar and should not be remembered as the person who canceled their meeting.

Scheduling Field Instruction

Another similar expectation is that you proactively arrange to meet with your field instructor for supervision, that you schedule your weekly sessions, and that you keep those appointments faithfully. A student's reliability includes submitting required process recordings and other documents designed to enhance field instruction at the arranged time, without being asked. Therefore, a reliable student should not put him or herself in a position of being chased after for these items. In other words, this is the best way to avoid creating any unprofessional noise or drama related to your student role.

Timeliness

It is important that a student does not leave other people waiting, even if it is believed that they do not notice. They notice. You do not want to be known as the social work student who has to be held accountable about lateness, chronic absenteeism, and excuses about how external events created a problem. Engage your self-awareness, and consider if it is productive for you to damage your reputation.

Assessing Your Work Ethic

Related to time management is the topic of your work ethic. *Merriam-Webster Collegiate Dictionary* defines *work ethic* (2015) as "a belief in work as a moral good." Companies believe that all employees need to be committed to hard work and excellence in order for a company or agency to succeed. From Ralph Lauren to nonprofit settings, all are required to exert 100% effort on behalf of service to clients, which includes reflection and going the extra mile to learn about skills that will provide the best service to that person.

Engage in self-reflection to gain understanding of your work ethic. First, assess the extent to which you have been prone to cutting corners in class in the past and now. Consider how these behaviors may carry over to your field work. If you have been doing this in your classes, it will carry over to field work. If you discover the stark truth that you have done the least amount required to pass your courses, it is cause for reconsideration. If in college, earning a C+ or a B grade was acceptable, this expectation in graduate school will make you a marginal student at best or a failing one at worst. Anything below a B is not a pass in social work programs. In the words of master chef Emeril Lagasse, "You have to kick it up a notch" (Emeril Lagasse, 2015) or two. Add the heavy cream, the extra syrup, and increased energy to your performance (Emeril Lagasse, 2015).

Collegiality and Flexibility Are Required

Demonstrating relatedness with others, like saying hello when walking by the nurses' station or to the security officer at the building's entrance is needed. This includes treating support staff in the office or the person at the coffee stand with respect and friendliness. One must remember that they are not invisible. As a student from Social Work University, you represent your program, not yourself. Everything you say and do reflects upon fellow students, everyone's potential to gain future employment, and your program's reputation in the community.

BARRIERS TO ACCEPTANCE BY THE AGENCY

Many possible pitfalls and minefields have been presented to show what agencies want and expect from students. In the process, much was discussed about what student behaviors can undermine their acceptance. Let's consider what barriers can impede student acceptance and/or functioning at the agency.

Being Self-Absorbed

A field work agency does not need a student who is absorbed in his or her skills. They want to know you are not using a filter related to your own view to understand your role.

CASE ILLUSTRATION 3.8

SELF-ABSORBED STUDENT LOSES PLACEMENT

Nora was unable to acknowledge that she had earned a C in her practice paper. She was argumentative with the professor and later reported to the associate dean that she

(Continued)

(Continued)

had been treated unfairly. Upon asking to see her papers, the associate dean immediately saw that they were poorly written. Her feedback to Nora included directing her to the university writing center. But Nora's inflated sense of her abilities got in the way. She did not take the advice to seek help from the writing center. The belief that she knew what she was doing led to her eventual dismissal from her field placement and loss of agency job in the site where her field placement was located. As a result, she was unable to complete first-year field work.

CASE ILLUSTRATION 3.9

DISORGANIZED STUDENT ASKED TO LEAVE PLACEMENT

Mike was placed at a nursing home for first-year field work. Despite being instructed to see certain residents on particular days and to write brief notes in their records on what transpired, he missed meetings with residents. His chart notes were also incomplete or omitted.

After three weeks, his field instructor worked with him in detail on what he had to do. In going over these details, she saw he was not taking notes. When she pointed this out to him, Mike said he would remember what she said. She told him directly that he did not remember.

Mike continued to not meet requirements. His field instructor contacted the school and let the field director know Mike was being asked to leave the placement.

Being Unfocused, Disorganized, Missing Deadlines

In another vein, an intern who is unfocused appears scattered or disorganized and one who does not meet deadlines is also undesirable.

Allowing Life to Get in the Way

Many students first starting a social work program bring life's complexities to school. A student may have a family whose care and sustainment he or she is responsible for. Another student has to hold down a job to keep afloat. A student has one

CASE ILLUSTRATION 3.10

STUDENT CARETAKER FOR ELDERLY MOTHER

Patricia's mother was elderly and quite frail. She lived with Patricia, who began to have many absences in field work because of her mother's needs. Her field instructor and faculty advisor worked with her to increase the supports she had in place for her mother during the time when she was at her field placement and in school.

Early on as a student, Patricia was encouraged to restructure her projected class schedule. In order for her life at home and in school to go smoothly, Patricia had to find courses that fit into her schedule and accommodated her mother's home care worker. As a result, she could not take courses from all the professors she wanted. However, because she was open to the advice, Patricia made compromises, which avoided crises and allowed her to finish the program.

family member, such as a disabled child, whose issues may get in the way. Social work schools recognize these constraints and try to work out a placement within a viable geographic location and time frame for the student. However, the student will have to meet requirements and ensure that he or she is not called away from field work for ongoing family and personal crises. The faculty advisor can help the student to determine a realistic plan for succeeding, usually requiring a compromise. Rather than relying on your initial plan, you must work out viable schedules and heed advice.

Trying to Renegotiate the Terms of Your Field Placement

The school's field office and the agency jointly plan and design the field placement assignments and the intern's schedule based on agency needs and the school's requirements. Students are expected to follow through with agencies by meeting a predetermined schedule and assignments and finalizing the schedule during the first week of field work. Any constraints must be presented to the field office before the student is assigned. It is generally not appropriate for the student to renegotiate the contractual relationship between the agency and the school. Any changes should be approved by the faculty field advisor and the field office before bringing them to the agency.

CASE ILLUSTRATION 3.11

SCHEDULING AN EXTRA "VACATION" TO MEET FAMILY OBLIGATION

Ingrid was a first-year student. She had met with a field office faculty member and was given information including the time frame for field work, holidays, start date, and spring break. All of the dates are placed on the calendar well before students begin field work. During the start of spring semester, she told her field instructor that she had scheduled an extra week beyond March spring break to attend a family event outside of the country. This had not been discussed with the faculty field liaison nor the field office. The field instructor called the field office, and the field director requested that Ingrid meet with him. It was strongly suggested to her that a two-and-a-half-week break would not be acceptable and that she needed to remain in field work through part of her spring break—in essence, trading spring break time for the following week since she was expected at the family affair.

CASE ILLUSTRATION 3.12

ADJUSTING CLASS DAYS TO ATTEND WEEKLY AGENCY MEETING

Oftentimes, agencies hold case conference meetings on a particular day of the week. Students are expected to attend. Karla told the educational coordinator at her initial interview that she could not come to field work on Wednesdays because she had scheduled classes on that day. She went to a field office faculty member to request a change of placement. The field faculty member instead explained to Karla that she must change her class schedule to accommodate field work and that policy allowed this change in schedule—even if classes are closed. The field faculty member called the agency and explained that Karla was relieved to learn that she could change her schedule to attend Wednesday meetings and was looking forward to the placement.

Dealing With Required Background Checks and Medical Documentation

More often than not, agencies require students to submit to background checks. Since the role of social worker and social work intern encompasses work with vulnerable clients: children, people with mental health issues, developmental disabilities, or levels of cognitive and physical impairment, it is essential that everyone who works with them has the integrity to do the job. When students are accepted by an agency, usually after an initial interview, they will meet with the human resources department and will present themselves to an agency for fingerprinting and a review of criminal records and arrest records. In addition, medical settings require documentation about a range of immunizations and some will ask for drug testing.

Several cautionary words: If there is an issue in your life that occurred prior to social work school or something current, this needs to be discussed with the field office. This must be done before agency assignments and meetings are made. For example, if you were in an abusive relationship and filed an order of protection against your abuser and your abuser counter-filed, this information will be discovered when the background check is conducted. Or you may not be a legal U.S. resident. Falsifying your background on any forms you complete at the agency constitutes clear grounds for being denied acceptance at the placement. Therefore, a student with a prior arrest record should not write no on the form asking the question, then submit to the background check, which will be returned as a failed test. Preventive measures must be taken by discussing these issues with the director of field education at your school.

One final cautionary word: You should note that in addition to asking for your physician to provide information about your immunizations, hospitals will have you submit to their own testing for medical clearance. Any use of recreational and other drugs will be detected and you will be denied the field placement—in addition to the embarrassment you will feel. There is absolutely no leeway here. Blaming the poppy seeds on the roll or bagel won't work if you failed the drug test. You will not have another chance.

Types of agencies that are apt to test you are those that serve children and people with disabilities or mental health diagnoses. Medical facilities also require medical clearance.

CASE ILLUSTRATION 3.13

STUDENT FAILS BACKGROUND CHECK

A first-year student, Wilma, withheld from the field office that she has an open case with Child Protective Services. She underwent a complex screening for the local children's services agency and failed the mandatory background check for a placement in a child protective setting.

CASE ILLUSTRATION 3.14

STUDENT FAILS DRUG TEST

Bonnie, a second-year student, was at a party and claimed she did not know what was in the cookies being passed around. She failed the drug test and lost a desirable medical placement and stipend that went with it. She was very weepy and embarrassed in telling the field director. The incident was used as a teaching moment, and Bonnie was reassigned.

SUMMARY

Being accepted by an agency requires your proactive involvement in making an impression as someone who is astute, mature, and trustworthy. A student who can follow directions and shows the ability to be responsible for his or her own learning is an optimal intern. Students have to show good verbal communication skills at an interview and solid writing skills in e-mails. Advanced materials such as forms and résumés need to be accurate and professional. Students' written materials have to demonstrate their ability to organize thinking and doing. In these initial phases, students have to show good judgment and maturity and the ability to adapt their social media, presentations, and voicemail greetings to this new career. Students must deal effectively with all aspects of screening, which include agency background checks and medical screenings.

Chapter 4 focuses on social work competencies that students are expected to develop in the field work experience.

Chapter 4

Developing Social Work Competencies

INTRODUCTION

Once accepted by an agency, you will undoubtedly start thinking about what you will be learning to do and what your outcomes will be by the end of foundation field work as a senior-year bachelor in social work (BSW) student or first-year master in social work (MSW) student. You may construct scenarios and what-ifs, trying to predict something about the year ahead. If excessive, these attempts can increase your anxiety while you believe these scenarios are having the opposite effect. You hope to gain control of a situation that is primarily not in your control. Starting field work is anxiety producing. You do not know what to expect of others, nor of yourself. Yet you want to do a good job. Try to keep your judgments about the placement to a minimum. Focus on your positive anticipation by envisioning who might need your help at this setting and what can be learned as a result.

This chapter provides you with two types of direction. The first very brief direction is designed to help you start off on the right foot by calming your anxieties and unproductive preoccupations. The second direction outlines social work competencies you are expected to develop by year's end to facilitate your understanding of where you are heading.

GETTING STARTED ON THE RIGHT FOOT AT FIELD PLACEMENT

You should get off to a good start when you show up at the agency on your first day and make a positive impression. This involves avoiding the hazards of making an unproductive entrance. You want to begin by greeting everyone with a simple hello. Report to where you have been told, and do not get sidetracked along the way. Let agency staff do their jobs. They will be focused on assigning a place for your belongings, showing you your desk, formally entering you into their system, and having you fill out their forms. Contain your anxiety. More often than you realize, your early questions will be about trying to understand the complexities of a situation that is not yet within your scope of knowledge. Learning about the agency takes place in a process.

Be aware that the agency is responsible for handling a student's entry. Your part is to follow their directives by going to the agency at the assigned day and time and doing what you are supposed to do when you get there. They will sign you in, set up an e-mail account and computer access, and provide any necessary trainings and orientations you will need. Once field work begins, you will have to stay focused on seeing clients as your most important priority, arranging field instruction, and quietly learning to develop mechanisms for survival. Questions about what you are going to learn will be met with answers about trusting in the process—usually because a full explanation of an occurrence not yet experienced is by its nature incomplete. The extent of your confusion will vary with your background. Just know that being puzzled is part of the process.

Soon you will begin the work of developing social work competencies through the integration of classroom learning and the field work experience.

FIELD EDUCATION AS THE "SIGNATURE PEDAGOGY" OF SOCIAL WORK

The recognition of the centrality of field work to the attainment of competency led to a policy declaration of great consequence to social work education. Read on, for further understanding.

In 2008, the Council on Social Work Education (CSWE; 2015) first adopted as policy that field education is the signature pedagogy of social work.

What is *signature pedagogy*? The concept of signature pedagogy comes from the field of philosophy and philosophies of education, which relate to all professions and how they meet their obligations to society (Shulman, 2005). Scholars at the Carnegie Foundation for the Advancement of Teaching (Gardner & Shulman, 2005), have endeavored to understand the nature of professional training in various fields. A crucial structure relevant to all professions is that of "signature pedagogy" as the means through which a profession socializes its students to its competencies, knowledge, and values (Shulman, 2005). For you, field education is the medium being used to involve you in developing the competencies, knowledge, and values of social work.

So, when starting to think "why am I being asked to do x, y, and z in my place-ment," the student has to bear in mind that the field education structures he or she is participating in have been developed and fine-tuned since Jane Addams and John Dewey. A field placement allows the student to work with assigned clients in an agency with a function and purpose. By way of field instruction (which is different from staff supervision), the student learns to enact the professional role, developing skill upon skill upon self-awareness and feedback.

There are three components of social work practice that students must learn. The first component, *performing,* involves action. The second component, *knowing,* refers to the body of scientific knowledge and research that informs professional action. The third component pertains to *integrating the professional values* that inform action (Shulman, 2005).

Performing

The CSWE (2015) has identified nine competencies of social work and the practice behaviors contained in these competencies. Schools have to evaluate stu-dents' competency attainment. All competencies are developed in the field experi-ence to varying degrees and in a relationship between the field experience and the classroom. Students primarily develop these competencies by applying knowledge values and self-awareness by engaging with clients and participating in the reflec-tive relationship with a field instructor. The performance of professional skills occurs by integrating self-reflection on a student's role with clients with active involvement in field instruction and the classroom.

To attain competency, a student will utilize the feedback loop with a field instructor, classroom learning, process recordings, and the Johari Window.

Knowledge for Practice

Knowledge gleaned from professional literature and research should always guide the student's performing role and the development of competency. Most relevant knowledge comes from the curriculum that is constructed by faculty and meets accrediting standards. The full BSW curriculum and first-year MSW stan-dards require learning social work's foundation areas and principles, focusing on practice, human behavior, research, social welfare organization, and cultural com-petence. Second-year MSW standards are focused on each school's curriculum that faculty design for specific areas of specialization.

Further knowledge for practice is acquired from the agency's practice domain. For example, a placement serving people with mental illness exposes a student to knowledge about that psychosocial problem, practice perspectives, policy impli-cations, and current research. The student will also have to consider how that knowledge is universally applicable to all of social work practice at the foundation level or the advanced second-year specialization.

Professional Values for Practice

Students learn the values and ethics of the profession in order to practice. The liberal arts foundation should provide the knowledge base for understanding values that underlie the practice of the social work profession. All professions are guided by values and ethics, as in medicine, law, accounting, and museum curatorship.

Thus, students in field work with clients must consider the ethical principles that guide their work and the values these ethical principles are based on. While client self-determination, for example, can be learned and its components studied in the classroom, its application becomes more complicated in actual practice with a client. Client self-determination requires the practitioner to facilitate a process fostering the client's independence, autonomy, and self-actualization. Yet, when facing real client situations with children or when a client's judgment is impaired and when self-determination infringes on others, you recognize that ethical decisions are highly nuanced. Another ethical dictum requires a nonjudgmental approach to clients, in order to provide fair and equitable services. To practice ethically, you must try to recognize your biases toward individual clients, which may or may not impair your practice.

SOCIAL WORK COMPETENCIES AND PRACTICE BEHAVIORS

The social work competencies you will be developing are comprised of practice behaviors and have as their foundation professional knowledge and values.

The nine competencies identified by the social work profession have to be developed by students during the course of professional education (CSWE, 2015). By the end of the foundation year, senior-year BSW and first-year MSW students should have developed these competencies to demonstrate competency attainment. Included are 29 suggested practice behaviors that reflect the competencies. Schools may develop their own unique practice behaviors that reflect competencies. By the end of the second advanced MSW year, students should have developed the competencies in further depth. Each school outlines practice behaviors specific to second-year concentrations; they identify the specifics of competencies through their curricula and evaluate students' attainment of them.

The nine competencies are provided for you to review to familiarize yourself with the path you are on and the goals you will have to meet. Competency attainment will be reviewed in depth in other chapters. For now, study them to gain an overview of where you are heading. These competencies may be amended in the next 10 to 30 years of your professional practice. That does not mean that the current competencies will be outdated. Rather, they may be revisioned as practices evolve, as social workers learn more about what is humanistic, and as they improve upon the implementation of professional values.

Competency 1: Demonstrate Ethical and Professional Behavior

The following practice behaviors demonstrate the attainment of competency. Social workers do the following:

- Make ethical decisions by applying the standards of the NASW (National Association of Social Workers) *Code of Ethics* (NASW, 2008), relevant laws and regulations, models for ethical decision making, ethical conduct of research, and additional codes of ethics as appropriate to context.
- Use reflection and self-regulation to manage personal values and maintain professionalism in practice situations.
- Demonstrate professional demeanor in behavior; appearance; and oral, written, and electronic communication.
- Use technology ethically and appropriately to facilitate practice outcomes.
- Use supervision and consultation to guide professional judgment and behavior.

Competency 2: Engage Diversity and Difference in Practice

The following practice behaviors demonstrate the attainment of competency. Social workers do the following:

- Apply and communicate understanding of the importance of diversity and difference in shaping life experiences in practice at the micro and macro levels.
- Present themselves as learners and engage clients and constituencies as experts of their own experiences.
- Apply self-awareness and self-regulation to manage the influence of personal biases and values in working with diverse clients and constituencies.

Competency 3: Advance Human Rights and Social, Economic, and Environmental Justice

The following practice behaviors demonstrate the attainment of competency. Social workers do the following:

- Apply their understanding of social, economic, and environmental justice to advocate for human rights at the individual and system levels.
- Engage in practices that advance social, economic, and environmental justice.

(Continued)

(Continued)

Competency 4: Engage in Practice-Informed Research and Research-Informed Practice

The following practice behaviors demonstrate the attainment of competency. Social workers do the following:

- Use practice experience and theory to inform scientific inquiry and research.
- Engage in critical analysis of quantitative and qualitative research methods and research findings.
- Use and translate research findings to inform and improve practice, policy, and service delivery.

Competency 5: Engage in Policy Practice

The following practice behaviors demonstrate the attainment of competency. Social workers do the following:

- Assess how social welfare and economic policies impact the delivery of and access to social services.
- Critically analyze and promote policies that advance human rights and social, economic, and environmental justice.

Competency 6: Engage With Individuals, Families, Groups, Organizations, and Communities

The following practice behaviors demonstrate the attainment of competency. Social workers do the following:

- Apply knowledge of human behavior and the social environment and practice context to engage with clients and constituencies.
- Use empathy, reflection, and interpersonal skills to effectively engage diverse clients and constituencies.

Competency 7: Assess Individuals, Families, Groups, Organizations, and Communities

The following practice behaviors demonstrate the attainment of competency. Social workers do the following:

- Collect, organize, and critically analyze and interpret information from clients and constituencies.

- Apply knowledge of human behavior and the social environment, person-in-environment, and other multidisciplinary theoretical frameworks in the analysis of assessment data from clients and constituencies.
- Develop mutually agreed-on intervention goals and objectives based on the critical assessment of strengths, needs, and challenges within clients and constituencies.
- Select appropriate intervention strategies based on the assessment, research knowledge, and values and preferences of clients and constituencies.

Competency 8: Intervene With Individuals, Families, Groups, Organizations, and Communities

The following practice behaviors demonstrate the attainment of competency. Social workers do the following:

- Implement interventions to achieve practice goals and enhance capacities of clients and constituencies.
- Apply knowledge of human behavior and the social environment, person-in-environment, and other multidisciplinary theoretical frameworks in interventions with clients and constituencies.
- Use interprofessional collaboration as appropriate to achieve beneficial practice outcomes.
- Negotiate, mediate, and advocate with and on behalf of clients and constituencies.
- Facilitate effective transitions and endings that advance mutually agreed-on goals.

Competency 9: Evaluate Practice With Individuals, Families, Groups, Organizations, and Communities

The following practice behaviors demonstrate the attainment of competency. Social workers do the following:

- Select and use appropriate methods for evaluation of outcomes.
- Critically analyze, monitor, and evaluate intervention and program processes and outcomes.
- Apply evaluation findings to improve practice effectiveness at the micro and macro levels.

Now that you have a basic picture of where you are going, consider that while competencies are generic to all of social work, they may translate uniquely within each school's curriculum and field manuals. Review your school's curriculum for further clarification as you proceed through field work.

SOCIAL WORK COMPETENCIES AND YOUR SCHOOL'S CURRICULUM: FOUNDATION FIELD WORK

You should be able to locate a list of competencies within your field curriculum. Look at your school's field work manual or its field work curriculum for its interpretation of the competencies and practice behaviors; it may also be found in a course outline for field work. Another place where you will immediately locate the measures of competence is in your school's field work evaluation. All expectations outlined by your school have been approved by the CSWE's accreditation process.

Interpretations of competencies will differ by level. First-year MSW students and senior-year BSW students are expected to develop the same competencies by the end of their field work. The competencies remain the same for second-year students, but the depth and focus will change.

To illustrate how schools may develop their own way of evaluating your competency attainment, some examples are included from several schools' foundation curricula.

CASE ILLUSTRATION 4.1

COMPETENCY 6: ENGAGE WITH INDIVIDUALS, FAMILIES, GROUPS, ORGANIZATIONS, AND COMMUNITIES

Practice Skills of Pre-Engagement (Wurzweiler School of Social Work [WSSW], 2014, p. 34)

"By the end of the first year, a graduate student should be able to: seek out and utilize appropriate sources of data in order to gain access to information about the client, change agent or target system" (WSSW, 2014, p. 34).

Included is the ability to "Integrate relevant data in ways that provide focus to initial understanding and exploration or concerns of client, change agent or target system" (WSSW, 2014, p. 34).

Practice Skills of Engagement and Exploration (WSSW, 2014, p. 37)

"By the end of first year, the student should be able to utilize a range of open ended questions which facilitate involvement and presentation of issues by members of client, client action, target, and action systems. . . ."

"Present oneself as a non-judgmental, professional individual. . . ."

"Demonstrate curiosity about the client as it originates from the presentation of the present situation and concern . . ." (WSSW, 2014, p. 37).

"Reach for indirect cues presented by client in individual or family sessions" (WSSW, 2014, p. 38).

CASE ILLUSTRATION 4.2

COMPETENCY 7: ASSESS INDIVIDUALS, FAMILIES, GROUPS, ORGANIZATIONS, AND COMMUNITIES

Practice Skills of Assessment (WSSW, 2014, p. 42)

With regard to assessment skills with individuals, "By the end of the first year the student should be able to begin a differential application of theory to guide and enable the formulation of a systematic assessment" (WSSW, 2014, p. 42).

With regard to assessment skills with groups, "By the end of the first year the student should be able to recognize that making an assessment of a group requires first an understanding of group rather than individual dynamics" (WSSW, 2014, p. 43).

CASE ILLUSTRATION 4.3

COMPETENCY 8: INTERVENE WITH INDIVIDUALS, FAMILIES, GROUPS, ORGANIZATIONS, AND COMMUNITIES

Practice Skills of Intervention With Individuals and Families (WSSW, 2014, p. 51)

"By the end of the first year the student should be able to use a range of skill with individuals and families to enable goal achievement. These include . . . Reframing

(Continued)

(Continued)

problems for individuals and families; utilizing universalizing and generalizing skills" (WSSW, 2014, p. 51).

Practice Skills of Intervention With Groups (WSSW, 2014, p. 52)

"By the end of the first year the student should be able to use support and sustainment skills to strengthen bonds, communication and supportive mechanisms. This includes eliciting from members reactions to other members' presentations" (WSSW, 2014, p. 52).

SOCIAL WORK COMPETENCIES AND YOUR SCHOOL'S CURRICULUM: SECOND-YEAR FIELD WORK

Competencies for second-year MSW students remain the same as in first-year field work. However, second-year performance is related to developing depth in competency attainment that is reflected in practice behaviors from the student's second-year concentration. These practice behaviors are designated by your school. Therefore, you should examine the practice behaviors of your chosen second-year concentration.

To give you a brief overview of where you may be heading, an illustration will be utilized from one school's evaluation of student performance in the second year.

CASE ILLUSTRATION 4.4

SCHOOL OF SOCIAL WORK IN THE NORTHEAST (2015)

This school of social work provides a list of social work's nine competencies that students are expected to attain. The school's first-year evaluation employs a Likert-type rating scale for field instructors to use in evaluating students' attainment of each practice behavior.

For second year, schools develop their own specializations. The same competencies apply with further depth and specificity. This school of social work provides a list of practice behaviors in the second year evaluation related to competencies students are expected to attain. The second year evaluation focusing on the specialization in clinical practice with individuals employs a Likert-type rating scale for field instructors to use in evaluating students' attainment of important practice behaviors.

For example, under ASSESSMENT, the evaluation states, "Develops a diagnostic impression utilizing relevant guidelines (agency or DSM IV)." (NYU Silver School of Social Work, 2015, p. 5).

Similarly, under INTERVENTION SKILLS for the same specialization, the evaluation states, "Differentiates between the range of normal development and behaviors and pathological adaptation." (NYU Silver School of Social Work, 2015, p. 6).

Further detailed discussion of competency attainment will be found in Chapters 9 and 10.

SUMMARY

Nine social work competencies identified by the social work profession have been provided to prepare you for the goals that you will have to meet. There are 29 practice behaviors that accompany these competencies, which must be fulfilled during a student's foundation year. In your second year, you will gain depth in the competencies by completing practice behaviors designed specifically for your concentration. This framework has been provided to put you on the path and create awareness of where you are heading in your foundation year and beyond.

Chapter 5 focuses on the educational relationship between student and field instructor.

Part II

The Design and Structure of Field Work

Chapter 5

The Relationship Between Field Instructor and Student

INTRODUCTION

Students need to have supervision from a qualified social worker in order to function effectively at their field placements. In that process, they must be open to learning, listening, and taking in perspectives from their field instructors. Students have to be honest about their work, expose limitations and mistakes, and show self-awareness.

Students' approaches to field instruction will vary. Some will be quite open to exposing their work and their self-awareness limitations. Usually, these students do not have many fears about revealing their limitations or do not maintain secrecy about their personal issues. Some students will be distrusting or guarded for fear that others will find out how little they know or personal information they do not want to expose. Other students may face difficulties maintaining boundaries with clients they identify with. They risk reliving a prior situation that causes stress and interferes with their work. They may seek crisis counseling in addition to supervision from their field instructor. A generally open and self-disclosing student, even one who occasionally blurs the boundaries between receiving field instruction and crisis counseling, is usually productive in the educational process with a field instructor and in the process with clients. A student's guarded behavior places clients at higher risk and compromises the field instruction relationship. The student who is open, honest, and able to show vulnerability and willingness to expose gaps or mistakes does not place clients at risk. The guarded student may give the field instructor cause to wonder if all that is discussed with clients is being reported and the extent to which the student's self-protection filter is preventing disclosure about difficulties being experienced with clients.

This chapter describes the roles of field instructor and student, highlighting important aspects of the coaching relationship. It also demonstrates the ethical necessity for maintaining honesty and openness in the interaction.

ROLES OF FIELD INSTRUCTORS

It is important to consider that, as a student, you are the person working with clients, not your field instructor. You are in the room with your clients, groups, families, and community representatives, and you are engaged in an intersubjective interaction with them. Since you are assigned to accomplish something for and with the client, you are the one who is responsible. It is primarily your feelings that are impacted in the process, and it is you who may have to work with a client you do not like or are frustrated by.

Since your field instructor cannot do the job for you, this section will discuss how he or she helps you to perform the skills and competencies required for that job.

Cultivating Communication and Assessing Progress

The best way to understand the field instructor's role is to consider the role of a coach. Like a coach, the field instructor guides, directs, and provides feedback to improve the student's skill (Schon, 1990). While being guided and directed, the student reflects and ponders new paradigms for enhanced conceptualization and action. Field instructors search for the most effective way to provide feedback and direction that will be understood by the student.

However, the coaching experience is not without its frustrations, which are caused by factors from both parties. Sometimes frustrations occur because the student and field instructor have not developed an effective pattern of communication. The field instructor should consider possible reasons for the lapses in communication and how to improve them. Perhaps the student is hearing a meta-message of criticism. Although the field instructor did not intend to criticize, recognizing this dynamic provides direction for reframing messages. Other times, miscommunication occurs when the student is not being proactive in the interaction. The field instructor will have to bring this to the student's attention in order to rechannel learning.

It is also possible that the field instructor has not accurately assessed the student's educational progress or ability, considering the student's skill to be more advanced than it actually is. The field instructor did not start where the student was. In this situation, the student must tell the field instructor that he or she needs more concrete direction and orientation than has been given.

Structuring Field Instruction

Think of field instruction as a regular class. It must be scheduled in a similar manner and planned for in advance by the student and field instructor at a regularly scheduled time. Try not to change the weekly time. Although the expectation is for the student to schedule field instruction, some students may require more orientation and structure to perform in this role. The field instructor may have to remind the student to schedule several field instruction meetings. This is a sign to raise your level of proactivity and increase the responsibility you take for your learning. Since this is a structured learning experience, not a freewheeling conversation, bring a pad or note-taking device. Your field instructor may remind you if are neglecting this task.

Evaluating and Developing Student Skills

Together, you and your field instructor review your work with clients and focus on the skills you are using to help them. He or she raises important issues with you, including required skills you have not yet tried, blind spots, or skills that are difficult for you to undertake. You may not feel that you are having difficulties with these skills or think that you know which ones are difficult for you. Consider why you may be having these reactions. More likely than not, it is because you want to appear competent to your field instructor, whom you respect or like or are a little bit afraid of. Field instructors usually understand that this is part of the learning process. Your coach is in a good position to give you the feedback you need to enhance the skills you have and to develop those you do not yet have.

For instance, imagine that after six weeks of meeting with your client Morris, you determine that he is not engaging with you. He skirts your questions and does not provide you with information. This relationship leaves you frustrated and uncertain about your effectiveness. On the other hand, you feel you are doing well with your client Jasmine, who reveals a great deal about herself in every session. First, try to determine how each client is making you feel. In the interaction with Morris, you feel anxious and also frustrated; in the interaction with Jasmine, you feel relieved and modestly capable. You talk with your field instructor about the last two sessions with Jasmine and share that you are not clear yet about your work with Morris. Your field instructor asks you to write a process recording of a meeting with Morris and one of a meeting with Jasmine. (See Appendix A for process recording outlines.) You do as instructed.

You talk about both process recordings in your next field instruction session, trying to delineate a step-by-step and word-for-word "he said, I said." Writing a process recording of a session with a client with whom you are not connecting will prove very helpful in figuring out what is going on between you. The process recording is a coaching tool. Together with your field instructor, you may frame an approach for you to try based on something you missed entirely. Your field instructor's feedback should open you up to unrecognized areas. You may see your inability to sit with the client's lack of openness. Or there may be something he has not yet told you that has to be shared.

The next step is to look at your blind spots. It is possible that development of skills will have to center on what you are not seeing about yourself in relation to this client. You may learn that the relief you experience in hearing Jasmine's revelations prevents you from giving her the focus and directions she needs. The client is talking. You feel competent; that is not enough.

Keeping the Student the Center of Attention

One important fact you have to understand is that in examining your work, your field instructor's primary center of attention is you—the student—not the client. The client is to be *your* center of attention. It's not that your field instructor ignores your client. He or she ensures that you are tending to the client appropriately. But your interventions and use of self are central in field instruction. Your field instructor will look for similarities in what goes on with you and Morris and with you and Jasmine. Discovering the common patterns in your practice with clients will enhance your understanding and approaches on how to proceed with each individual. You may find that the comfort you feel with Jasmine is a deterrent, preventing you from being critical of your role with her. The reality is that you need to do something different with her beyond what you are doing. On the contrary, your discomfort with Morris is working out in your favor as a learner. Although Morris's pace makes you anxious, you realize he is involved with you and never misses appointments. You conclude further that you have to accept his pace.

Your field instructor advises you to focus Jasmine on her issues. Your next two process recordings reveal that instead of providing focus for her, you tend to let her go on and on. In discussion it emerges that you do not know how to redirect her ventilations and take charge of the meeting. You interpret her talking as a good sign of involvement. Two issues have to be addressed in order for you to develop further practice skills. The first is to learn to refocus her, which may include gentle interruption. The second is to hone your skills of actively listening to her. You will do this by identifying the themes she talks about and prioritizing them as they relate to your earlier joint contracting with her. Then you need to consider how to present back to her what you are hearing. In the process, you discover you were not such a great listener after all; this is how you improve your listening skills.

As a result of the coaching experience with regard to these clients, you have learned the need for active listening, focusing and prioritizing, and gently interrupting clients as well as how to move at the client's pace. Remember the Johari Window (Luft & Ingham, 1955) discussed in Chapter 1? It describes the feedback loop that comes about in field instruction. Figure 5.1 depicts how your field instructor's feedback expanded your understanding of your role with Jasmine.

Assessing Competency Development and Learning Style

The educational assessment is an evolving picture of the student's progress in his or her development of practice skills, professional demeanor, and social work competency. The educational assessment also shows changes in the student's learning style.

One task of the field instructor is to construct an educational assessment about your progress in competency attainment. Up until now in this example, your field instructor has helped you see your need to work on active listening, harnessing

Figure 5.1   Johari Window—How Feedback Expands the Public Area

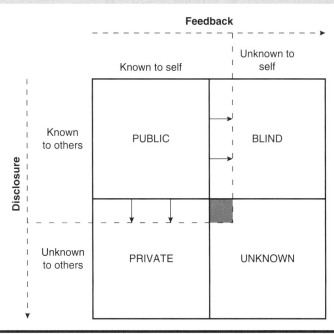

your anxiety, working within a client's pace, gently interrupting a client to provide focus to a session, and using active listening to prioritize a client's issues.

In addition, the field instructor recognizes your particular learning style—what is most effective in your learning. You have produced candid and thoughtful process recordings. A conclusion might be that you learn through candor and self-disclosure. However, another student in a master in social work (MSW) program that does not require process recordings may be more reluctant to write them. As a result, the field instructor experiences the student as defensive or guarded and finds it harder to point out that the student is not listening actively. The field instructor may assess the student's learning style to be hesitant about risking exposure. In this case, the field instructor will encourage the student to write a process recording. As a result, the student may reach the conclusion herself that she was not actively listening. A once-reluctant student may find comfort in being able to speak openly after sharing a process recording in the field instruction relationship.

Finally, it must be noted that blind spots are inherent in the work and are not a failing in the student. Learning is about creating structures in your own practice that allow blind spots to be identified.

Also knowing the stages in the student's learning is helpful in the field instruction process. The reluctance and fear of getting started (Reynolds, 1942) presented in Chapter 1, Stage 1: Acute Self-Consciousness, eventually gives way to Stage 2: Sink or Swim. The various attempts the student makes to arrive at the second stage require normalization by the field instructor as a universal part of the learning experience. Stage 3 involves knowing what to do but not always being able to do it. This stage carries students through their bachelor in social work (BSW) and MSW programs.

Serving as Role Model and Mentor

A role model is someone who provides an example to another in a particular area. Social work students look to professionals with whom they come in contact as exemplars in their performance of a professional role. They hope to find people whose behavior in executing their social work roles they can copy. Students also look to these role models for guidance, direction, and clues on how to think about clients and the profession and how to act.

A student just starting on his or her professional career will look for mentorship from a field instructor. In addition to providing opportunities for emulation, mentors should give clear guidance and direction on present and future actions. While classroom faculty are available and students experience mentorship relationships throughout their program, it is in the relationship with the field instructor that the role modeling opportunity has the most impact. The field instructor is normally the closest person to the environment in which the student will be working when he or she finishes the program. The new graduate will work in an agency providing services not all that different from those the field work is currently offering, in which he or she will be involved with agency staff, collateral contacts, and interdisciplinary models.

As a student you should try to consider what your field instructor has to offer to you in that role. He or she may or may not be close to you in age, desires, and values. It will be necessary for you to find your field instructor's strengths and positive attributes that you consider worthy of emulating regardless of your differences or similarities. It is equally important to factor out the qualities you do not find desirable, interesting, or admirable or those that you do not want to copy in pursuit of your own career path. Realistically understanding that you will not find someone whose full complement of behaviors and qualities you will wish to emulate allows you to maximize learning.

ROLES OF STUDENTS

Since you are directly responsible for the relationship with your clients, how you undertake the student role within the field instruction relationship will have profound

CASE ILLUSTRATION 5.1

FIELD INSTRUCTOR DEVOTED TO CLIENT WORTH AND DIGNITY

In the senior center where you are placed, your field instructor is fully devoted to the elderly participants. She connects them with frail, homebound elderly in the community in a way that you find admirable. She makes certain they receive a phone call, have meals delivered, and when someone on staff is not doing his or her job, she takes a strong position. You have heard her saying to a worker, "Our seniors deserve our fullest respect. You did not give them respect when you missed the visit." What you have learned is that all clients have worth and a right to your best service. You have learned to value what seniors bring and the full range of their histories through the relationship with your field instructor and her adamant insistence that staff provide the highest quality of care.

impact on your practice with clients. The level and quality of your engagement and proactivity with your field instructor will be major in defining the development of skills that will impact your work. Openness to being coached and critiqued will have to be developed, which includes asking for and being able to receive constructive feedback. Utilizing the structures of field instruction in a proactive manner will build your skill set. You also have to acknowledge your own tendency to want to be seen as competent if this prevents learning. You will have to accept anxieties about having your practice reviewed through process recordings and being evaluated.

Dealing With Practice Challenges in the Context of Your Inexperience

One of the major drawbacks encountered by students involves feeling vulnerable when realizing that there is much that you don't know. Yet this phenomenon is the best protection for a student because it serves one major purpose—these feelings safeguard the client from your lack of expertise. These mind-sets bring you to field instruction, frame your questions, give you pause to reconsider, and to think about how to act.

First, it is necessary for the beginning student to understand the context of the client. At the start, step back and consider your client—his or her context, stage in the life cycle, social history, present needs, and important issues. Knowing the community and its demographics allows you to more readily ascertain the person's place in it.

It will be necessary for you to understand who you are and your potential impact on your client. Preparatory empathy was discussed earlier as putting yourself in the client's shoes in order to grasp how to make a connection. Then, it becomes necessary to ponder how your own presentation might impact the client and how to prepare for any client concerns. Think about how your gender, age, cultural presentation, race, accent, and affect will be viewed by the client.

CASE ILLUSTRATION 5.2

A JEWISH STUDENT WHO WEARS A YARMULKE

Aaron is a 24-year-old Jewish student who wears a yarmulke. In his preparation for beginning with a school-age boys group of mixed ethnicities, he expressed concerns to his field instructor about how the boys will react to him. She suggested that in his introduction he tell the group he is a student and that he is also Jewish and that is why he wears a yarmulke. Then to ask the group to introduce themselves and to see if they have any religious or ethnic differences or attributes they would like to share.

She told Aaron to look for underlying confusion and to be aware they may want to ask questions since most of them do not know Jewish people.

Aaron shared that he is anxious because although he is used to mixed neighborhoods, having attended an urban university and lived in a diverse neighborhood, he is uncertain about how the kids will feel about him and how he will handle himself with them. Aaron wants to learn about them, and his field instructor encouraged him to use his curiosity to obtain information. By asking them, she noted, he will demonstrate to them that it is okay for them to ask.

Discussion

This illustration brings the discussion back to the Socratic (7th century BCE) dictum, "Gnothi seauton"—know thyself. If you are a 50-year-old African American male student with a group of men who were formerly incarcerated, you should prepare for assumptions group members may have of you. If you are a 50-year-old white male student with the same group, their beliefs about you will undoubtedly differ. A female student's race will be perceived differently depending on the client and perception will vary according to her age, clothing, and other factors of her appearance. Knowing who you are is not only about how you react. Recall the Johari Window (Luft & Ingham, 1955) from earlier chapters. Knowing who you are includes understanding what others know about you that you do not know about yourself. Included here is how you will be perceived as you engage clients.

Openly Contributing to the Coaching and Critiquing Process

It does not matter if you have been competent in another field or if you had to show only good qualities and hide your mistakes at a previous job. Field instruction does not work this way. Your most productive approach is to embrace the role of student. Remember, it is a luxury you will never have again. Resolve to consume everything your field instructor has to offer, and bring questions, concerns, and blunders to him or her.

CASE ILLUSTRATION 5.3

BRINGING AN INCIDENT WITH A CLIENT TO FIELD INSTRUCTION—OR AVOIDING

Your client's decision to never speak to her sister again caused you great anxiety. You cannot imagine never talking to your own sister again. You told your client you

(Continued)

(Continued)

would like to help her resolve these negative feelings. Your client told you no and changed the subject. Now you feel guilty that you turned off your client. On the other hand, you believe it is not good for her to harbor so much negativity toward her sister.

Now what? What should you do next? You aren't sure how you will present this to your field instructor. Then again, you are mad at yourself, and you do not want to present it to your field instructor. You discussed this with your close friend in the program. He affirmed that you should bring it to your field instructor and then asked, "What if the client's sister stole her money or harmed her in some other way? Why would your client ever have to talk to her sister again?" You never thought of it that way.

You decide to tell your field instructor about the incident in your weekly meeting, and you immediately feel relieved.

Understanding the Nature of the Coaching Process

After your field instructor listened to you recount the incident, she asked you about your own relationship with your sister. You said it is a positive and interdependent one. However, you have come to recognize that your relationship cannot be the model for all sibling relationships. You discover that you were unable to explore the client's concerns because you prejudged the situation based on your own experience. Your field instructor has requested that you consider how you might approach the client at your next meeting, and you have decided to revisit the topic by admitting to the client that you missed the chance to speak with her about the situation because of your own personal views and that you realize she must have a real reason to be upset with her sister.

Bringing the issue to field instruction enabled you to receive the necessary coaching to allow you to proceed further. Coaching involved asking you about your own sister. This allowed you to see how you imposed your own bias about sibling relationships, which closed down the exchange between you and your client. Coaching further involved asking you to develop a plan for the next client appointment, which you created and discussed in your field instruction meeting. As a result of the coaching, you execute the plan at your next client meeting.

When you meet your client again, you apply what you learned in the feedback process. Now you have learned something about how your biases might get in the way and cause you to shut down a client. Moving forward, other issues will emerge and other skills will have to be developed. They will be developed

Figure 5.2 Feedback Loop

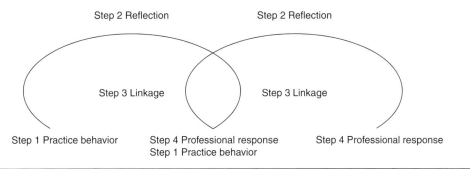

Source: The Practice of Field Instruction in Social Work: Theory and Process, 2nd edition, by Marion Bogo and Elaine Vayda. © University of Toronto Press 1998. Reprinted with permission of the publisher.

through the same coaching process—using the feedback loop, which is presented in Figure 5.2 (Bogo & Vayda, 1998).

Using Process Recordings to Deepen Feedback

While some schools require students to submit two process recordings weekly for review in field instruction, others do not. These are useful and important tools for heightening students' self-awareness, clinical skill, reflection, and application of theory to practice. The use of process recordings has a long history that comes from recognizing the significance of subtleties and latent content in practice. Process recordings are important catalysts in the feedback loop.

If you are writing them regularly, you are used to guided and directed self-disclosure. If not, you will probably feel more vulnerable at the outset, but this feeling will pass. It will become routine and you will become more open. Try it. Use one of the formats in Appendix A, and see what you discover from your interactions. The process recording adds a critical step in the development of skill. First, you have the client interaction. Then you record it, capturing the sequence and flow. After that, you bring it to field instruction for review and feedback. Through your joint dialogue, you are more quickly able to reflect on your actions and connect them to theory. Newer perspectives emerge along with further interventions, and the feedback loop continues.

Writing a process recording is a proactive undertaking that enhances your field instructor's coaching. Perhaps a parallel is the batter first reviewing a video of his at bat, hitting pause at crucial times, and then reviewing it with the hitting coach so that they can determine the subtleties in his movements that are causing the strike-outs. In this case, a verbal description of his at bat would be far less effective than the video and subsequent joint discussion. By the same token, the student's verbal presentation of the client session is less effective than the analysis of a process recording, which provides more data for review and learning.

CASE ILLUSTRATION 5.4

PROCESS RECORDING FROM A SECOND-YEAR STUDENT WITH SCHOOL-BASED BOYS' GROUP

This is my ninth meeting. The boys are supposed to focus on school and family issues. Eight members are present—Jake, Keetan, Andrew, Nathaniel, Gavin, Louis, Miguel, and Victor.

I thought about each boy's issues from the last meeting. I recalled my own difficulties in school with certain kids and my mom advocating for me.

I started the meeting by reminding them we had talked last week about family and how families express feelings. I asked if they had stuff to talk about. After silence and then laughter, and more silence, I said, "I know that you have feelings about family. Perhaps someone has an incident to talk about."

Jake jumped in and said he is angry at his brother because his mom always asks him to help Jake with homework. But his brother is impatient and yells at him. Jake says his mom wants him to do well like his brother. He says it makes him mad. I am so glad he talked about this because he acts out in class and doesn't get his work done. He is falling behind.

I asked them if others had conflicts at home with family. The boys talk about how some are know-it-alls who just tell you what to do. Louis says he has to follow his father's rules at home. Andrew laughs and says, "But you don't listen to teachers here, and you always get put on detention. Why? It's so effed up." They all laugh.

I pointed out that it looks like they have conflict at home. What about in school, with kids or teachers? To this, Keetan reports that his sister bosses him around—to get his homework done or she won't let him watch TV. Jake asks why she can get away with giving orders. Keetan then defends his sister. They get into a long discussion about bossy siblings. Some say that they should not let their sibs get away with things.

Following up on that Jake stated, "You get people to listen if you yell at them." A couple of kids found that pretty odd and said, "That's messed up." They talked more about yelling or not yelling. Then I asked, "How else can you get others to listen?" Someone said that having things explained to them works. Then they listen. They seemed to agree with that concept, and they liked that. They said they would listen more if things were explained to them.

I became concerned here because some of them were quiet. I wondered to myself if that's how they are at home, and I wanted to get at that. I said, "So it's great to have everyone looking out for you. But does anyone just go to his room and close the door?" Gavin, who doesn't say much, told the group that is what he does. He tries to stay out of his family's way.

It was too bad that it ended, but the period was up. I quickly said, "We can pick up next week. You guys have been so interesting today with what you shared. It's so important to understand what bugs us at home and to figure out what we can do to keep things on track with the family."

Impressions

I didn't like that the ending was so abrupt. I felt they were connecting and trusting each other a lot. I have been hearing they are doing a little better in their classes—calmer and more focused. That's great because in the group each kid is alert and focused. They don't drift out, even the quiet ones.

Plans for Future Action

I am going to try to keep them focused on sharing important issues and help them support one another.

Questions

Do you have activities to suggest that will involve them all?

CASE ILLUSTRATION 5.5

FIELD INSTRUCTION MEETING TO REVIEW PROCESS RECORDING

The field instructor, Penny, began their meeting by asking Willie, the student, how he felt in the meeting. Willie said he felt very connected to the boys. She agreed that she could see that. He said they seemed to be in the intimacy stage and liking and trusting each other. They were cohesive. Penny credited him for understanding the theory. She asked if he thought they were moving into a deeper stage to deal with harder issues. Willie said he wasn't sure. But since they will be together all year, he anticipates many more issues coming up.

Penny asked what it was like for Willie to ask the question about family. He said he was nervous about asking them to talk about family incidents. It felt almost too intrusive, even though they had talked about it previously. Penny asked, "How do you see the outcome of that question?" He said he was very pleased that he could do it and that they brought up many issues. Penny added a supportive comment

(Continued)

(Continued)

about taking the risk. Willie said it was a great interaction—talking about siblings and being bossed by others.

Penny wondered why Willie did not follow up on Jake's discussion about his mother wanting him to do as well as his brother. Willie said that he wanted the other kids to talk rather than focusing on Jake. She agreed that was a good group work technique. She said, "But this is something you remember and file away so you can return to it at a time when the others are closer to the same issue."

Penny asked, "How did you come to ask the group if others just withdraw from family interactions?" Willie replied, "I think it was because I knew some kids who did that and it really was a major issue. I knew a girl who used to binge eat and then purge just to withdraw from the family. I knew another kid who used to drink in his room." Penny said that she thought it was a terrific strategy to ask that question. She discussed the fact that Willie's comment helps develop a norm that it is permissible to be on different sides of an issue. So here, it's not just the kid who has outright family conflict who gets to talk; it's also giving permission to the kid who doesn't interact in the same way to talk. Willie said he hadn't thought of it in terms of a norm. She suggested he read more chapters on group work.

Penny asked, "When they talked about being bossed and Louis following orders at home but not in school, what did you make of that?" Willie said that Louis has an authority issue. Penny asked how he responds to Willie. He said that Louis wants to please him. She asked Willie to consider how the other kids respond to him. "I think they like me." Penny agreed and said, "But you are an authority figure to them. How do they respond? Louis wants to please you, but what about the others?" Willie said he hadn't thought about that. Penny suggested he write a few notes on that for next time and think about that as he works with the group in the next few sessions. He agreed.

She asked him about the abrupt ending. "How did you feel about the way you summarized the meeting?" He said under the circumstances—bells ringing—he didn't have much choice. She agreed that it is less of a problem since the group is ongoing and has a rhythm by now.

Discussion

First, in taking note of her coaching, Penny raises Willie's awareness of questions he posed to the group. This fosters the development of his conscious use of self. Then she asks him to consider how he was feeling. She points out some concepts that pertain to the group's progress at that time that he has not referred to. She helps him connect group theory to what he is doing by bringing up two group work concepts: group norms and the worker's authority. All of these issues give him further learning opportunities and will build his skill set. Willie will have a whole academic year with the kids, and this is only session 9.

Curbing Your Unenthusiastic Approach to Criticism

Everything that happens represents a teaching moment. Think of it this way: You are enrolled in a program to receive the attention and feedback from people far more experienced and learned in their profession than you are. Take full advantage of it. However, the trade-off is that you will have to restrict any hypersensitivity that you have. If you find yourself becoming defensive against criticism most of the time, start reflecting upon your prior relationships with authority, including parents, guardians, teachers, or doctors—those in your life who have had some power or control over you. It is up to you to figure this out. Get help if you have to. You can start by talking to a fellow student but not to a friend who is not a social worker. They will not know how to advise you about something so technically related to your profession. If you ask a chemist friend for accounting advice, you would have to take that advice with caution. You would be far better off if you asked an accountant. However, professional help may be warranted.

Getting on Board With the Procedures and Systems at Field Placement

Some of you may not like the idea of compliance to structures, systems, data entry, and designs. You still have to get on board. Everything has to be completed on time and done well. Your writing, spelling, conceptualizing, and paying attention to detail have to be at least "very good." Excellent is better. Anything below that is marginal and generally not acceptable. Of course, there are some things to be done that you may not like much, such as documentation. Documentation indicates that your agency provided the service paid for by tax dollars and foundations' donors. Your field instructor will evaluate you on these skills and prod and coach you when necessary.

Scheduling Regular Appointments for Field Instruction

Put all scheduled appointments in your appointment book, and make sure you keep them and show up on time. Have a regular meeting time, and try to keep it faithfully.

Bring agenda items and questions to field instruction for each session and take notes. Although messy and at times unpredictable, field work is a course you are taking. Keeping track of your notes as well as skill and competency development is useful. Students who have saved their notes throughout the entirety of their field placements usually marvel at their results a year or two later.

Recognizing and Accepting the Challenges of the Evaluation Process

Teachers, professors, field instructors, and most educators try to help students through the anxiety-producing aspects of being evaluated, graded, and judged.

Although it is important to allow yourself not to give in to fears and anxieties about being judged throughout your learning process, nonetheless, issues about being appraised will be heightened during evaluation time. Your need to be perfect—a high-achieving student with a history of excellent grades—will impede your openness to evaluative feedback related to gaps and skills to be developed. Or perhaps your prior negative experiences in educational settings will cause you so much anxiety you will be unable to rise to the occasion and take in feedback about what you still need to learn.

If extreme anxieties persist and begin to impede further learning, it is important that you figure out how to manage these feelings. If these reactions continue to be unmanageable, getting professional help to overcome the barrier to your advancement may be necessary.

CASE ILLUSTRATION 5.6

STUDENT'S TIMIDITY NEGATIVELY AFFECTS WORK WITH CLIENT AND IMPACTS FIELD INSTRUCTION

Olivia has an educational history filled with anxiety. She saw a therapist in middle school because she was shy and bullied. This affected her grades and friendships. She went to college still somewhat withdrawn but not as self-doubting. However, in the social work program her timidity has shown up again, and she has not been able to be proactive.

Her field instructor has been working on this with her. Her process recordings show she is asking open-ended questions, but once the client reveals herself in response to the question, Olivia does not follow through with further exploratory responses. She resists hearing her field instructor's feedback and becomes overwhelmed. However, in a future crisis with a client she sees that her lack of probing led to the client's inability to deal with her son's crisis in a timely manner. This created a family crisis.

Olivia wishes these requirements could be easy for her—that she did not have to struggle so much. This is part of why she doesn't always want to hear anything negative from her field instructor.

Olivia returns to therapy after the fall semester to work on her timidity in exploring topics further with clients. Her field instructor supports her decision and credits her for the great effort she is making to learn how to be an effective social worker. Her ability to hear feedback from her field instructor improves.

Discussion

This is an example of how a student's history of difficulty in the educational process reappears, just when the student thought it had been overcome. This difficulty takes the form of guardedness and inability to hear evaluative feedback. This reaction is strongest when under stress and she is very anxious when engaged in complex emotional interactions with clients that may become overwhelming.

SUMMARY

This chapter explained the roles of a field instructor as your coach and evaluator. It also focused on your role in the feedback process required in a field instruction relationship. The field instructor ultimately evaluates your skill development and helps you to grow in your competencies by discussing new skills, possible blind spots, or areas that you may struggle in. Part of the student's responsibility is to take it all in, accept feedback, be self-aware, and use the field curriculum and learning process to be open to growth and improvement.

Chapter 6 provides an analysis of how process recordings and other educational tools can be used to enhance practice and deepen competency attainment, self-awareness, and use of self.

Process Recording and Other Educational Tools

INTRODUCTION

The field placement experience provides a structured and systematically designed learning opportunity where the student develops social work skills and attains competencies. While classroom learning utilizes written papers, exams, and readings as educational tools, field work utilizes field instruction and process recordings as its primary learning tool for sharpening critical thinking and demonstrating competency. This chapter focuses on process recording and other formats as educational tools for the field placement experience.

PURPOSE OF PROCESS RECORDING

The major purpose of a process recording is to increase a student's ability to reflect on an interaction from practice. The progression in writing this document facilitates the learning and teaching experience in field instruction. Reviewing a process recording in the field instruction conference allows the student to enhance use of self in strengthening the relationship with the client and honing the development of skills in gathering, organizing, and reporting important data about interactions with a client or clients. In writing and reviewing a process recording, the student will consider theory applicable to the unique client situation. The document should be seen as a draft, an evolving work in progress that is never fully completed.

The process recording is a narrative presentation of your interaction with a client or client system. It tells the story of the interaction, whether the meeting is with a group, an individual, community members, or a family. Schools will provide preferred outlines for process recordings, and you will see several variations in this chapter. Whatever the outline, you will be asked to describe the interaction—include quotes; write what you said, what the client said, and what group or family members said; and identify each member. In addition, identifying themes of the meeting and considering relevant theory enhances learning. Including your feelings and reactions to clients' statements, needs, and feelings will deepen your understanding of the client.

The process recording is not like a formal paper handed to a professor for a grade. It is a teaching tool to be reviewed jointly with your field instructor to facilitate use of self and reflection. The process recording belongs to you the student, as well as your field instructor, agency educational coordinator, faculty advisor, and school. It is not a public document for agency files, future field placements, or future employers.

OUTLINE FOR NARRATIVE PROCESS RECORDING

One common format is the five-part narrative format. (See Appendix A for further common process recording formats.) This is used to strengthen the student's ability to grasp the holistic nature of the client's story and to integrate the student's observations into the narrative.

Part I: Pre-Engagement

In this section, the student describes how he or she prepared to meet with the client(s). Utilizing pre-engagement skills to prepare for a client meeting sharpens understanding that will enhance the connection with clients. The literature on pre-engagement, which is reviewed in foundation practice courses, provides two dimensions of pre-engagement.

1. The first dimension of pre-engagement is gaining knowledge of the situation. The student seeks out relevant data about the client and reviews important aspects of his or her situation. Having a client with a mental health or medical diagnosis necessitates researching the disease and symptoms to better understand what he or she is facing. If the client is a Somalian refugee family, the student should find out what the political and warring conflicts have been in that country.

2. The second dimension of pre-engagement is preparatory empathy. This requires that the student put himself or herself in the client's shoes. Watching the news can show a student what it is like to escape from a military conflict or from famine and disease. If a student is working with a parents' group but is not a parent, considering how he or she would feel having a child with a disability strengthens the client connection. For another example, a senior center's environment committee plans to lobby the state legislature to pass a bill that more strictly regulates dumping in a downstate river. A student has to imagine what it feels like to be a motivated senior with concern about the environment.

These skills will carry the student far in effectively meeting clients' needs. Therefore, it is necessary for a student to write how he or she prepared for a client meeting.

Part II: Narrative

The student then provides a narrative description that tells the story of the interaction and includes some details about who said what to whom, using quotes when warranted.

Although "verbatim recall" may be requested, in reality it does not exist. As the student gains experience in writing process recordings, his or her ability to accurately report interactions will improve. Quotes, observations, feelings, and connections to relevant theories that stand out should be included. While writing the process recording, the student will notice that he or she missed important content or may conclude, "I should have said something supportive here." This discovery of overlooked material occurring in the midst of the session is natural. That is how learning occurs. In short, writing the narrative exposes a student's "mistakes" and omissions.

When a meeting involves more than one client, the interactional dynamics are important to recognize and review. Theoretical material from class and readings about group, family, and community interactions and the social worker's role will provide the necessary fundamental information. Paying attention to group and family themes, empowerment issues, and recognizing which members are connected positively to each other and which ones are not enhances the work. These dynamics are important to know about families and groups and also vital in understanding community matters.

Summarizing throughout the narrative works well. "We had been talking about her son's learning issues and solving those problems within the school. We then went on to talk about her husband's differing approach to the child's learning situation . . . ."

Since social workers focus on client self-determination and are required to suspend value judgments, a student has to recognize personal values that conflict with those of the client and the extent to which his or her biases and judgments impede the work with clients. These become visible within the narrative presentation. For example, in one process recording, the student discovers that her personal bias brought about using her own agenda rather than supporting that of the client. Using the process recording to see when biases interfere is the student's best safeguard for giving the client fullest consideration. It is natural for students to have biased reactions and to deal with their value conflict dilemmas. It is problematic for clients when students do not recognize their biases and judgments.

This narrative material from process recordings provides excellent learning tools for field instruction.

Part III: Impressions

One or two brief paragraphs are written about how the student felt the meeting went. It contains the student's feelings about the client and what was accomplished. This summary reaction will provide the student and field instructor with an overview that will guide the joint meeting for field instruction.

Part IV: Plans for Future Action

This portion of the process recording guides students' development of habits for practice to be used in their future role as a professional. The student should write his or her thoughts about next steps, including advocacy tasks and how to work with the client in the next few meetings.

Critical thinking is heightened through reflections. In this way, the student develops the ability to think on his or her feet about the role with the client. A student will not necessarily follow up on all plans. Consideration of future action will be informed by the student's interaction with the field instructor.

Part V: Questions

To be an active learner, it is important for the student to frame questions to ask the field instructor while reviewing the client meeting. Both field instructor and student use their agendas to understand the student's process recording and engage in the feedback process.

Now that you understand the parts to the outline, you can see its use in action in some case illustrations.

CASE ILLUSTRATION 6.1

PROCESS RECORDING OF A FIRST-YEAR STUDENT WITH MOTHER OF TWO-YEAR-OLD

Pre-Engagement

In thinking about my client Ms. Daniels, I focused on her problems with her two-year-old child's behaviors and that she doesn't seem to know much about child development. I am not sure how to convey some of these theories to her in a way that won't make her feel defensive. But I have to help her be more patient with her son.

She has been talking about the recent lack of intimacy with her husband. This is a topic I had not expected since we were supposed to work on parenting issues. I prepared for handling this topic by talking to my field instructor. I am not sure how much to ask her, and asking about such personal matters already makes me anxious. It is not easy for me to put myself in Ms. Daniels's shoes because I am not married nor do I have any children. My field instructor suggested I let her talk and that I probe slowly and at my own comfort level. If she requires psychotherapy or couples counseling, we may refer her elsewhere.

Narrative

Ms. Daniels apologized for being late—the traffic was bad. She then stated that she was having problems with her son. He is now climbing all over everything, and she reported "constantly yelling at him to stop." I asked her why she wanted him to stop climbing, and she said "to give me peace." I asked if it were not possible for her to relax and just make sure he doesn't hurt himself. Ms. Daniels said he used to be "good" before he started walking. I suggested that his climbing was a natural development, and he needed to feel his way around—that he was growing and changing. Ms. Daniels laughed and said perhaps she should let him climb and just try to control him when they were in someone else's house. I said, "Okay, this is a start." She heard what I said. I agreed and laughed with her.

Ms. Daniels then began talking about her husband; he was staying out late and not calling her. I asked her what he said he was doing. She said his excuses were probably valid—work situations or extra meetings, and he couldn't make a call or text at those meetings. She said she did not believe there were other women, that they both take marriage seriously.

(Continued)

(Continued)

Ms. Daniels said she had argued with her husband this morning when he told her he bought a monthly rather than a weekly train ticket. I asked why this bothered her, and she started talking about bills again.

I asked Ms. Daniels if there was a realistic money problem—were they actually overspending? She said that there was enough money to cover bills but that her husband withheld money from her—that perhaps he should bring lunch to work to give her extra money. She said she might need debt counseling and not this counseling. I asked her if she thinks it was the money or if something else was bothering her. Ms. Daniels said her husband's staying out late bothered her. I asked if she thought he was staying out late to be away from her (she had mentioned that he also went to bars for socialization, not for actual drinking). She said maybe he stayed out because of the sex thing. I asked her to explain. Ms. Daniels said that she had gotten a urinary tract infection when they were first married and sex was painful; she had become afraid to have intercourse, and her husband got annoyed with her. I asked if she had gotten the UTI again. She said no. Also a few weeks ago, she hurt her back and could not have sex for a while. Ms. Daniels said they had sex last night, and it was good. I could not figure out why they would argue the next morning. I should have asked more about that. Maybe it is her fear of intimacy.

In a general way, I asked her to think about whether she was focusing too much on money—that perhaps this was pushing away her husband. She said maybe—that when they were at a church marriage encounter a couple of months ago and he began to open up, but she kept talking about money. I pointed out that she does this often—brings it back to money.

At the end of the session Ms. Daniels again asked if she should be in debt counseling instead of counseling. I said if she felt money was truly the problem I could refer her for debt counseling, but she should give some serious thought as to whether money was the issue. She said she would think about this during the week and see me next Friday. If she realizes why she focuses on money, we can begin to work on some of her reasons for pushing her husband away.

Impressions

I was surprised that we were getting to sexual issues so quickly. It made me anxious but not to the extent that I had anticipated. I think because she seems to be able to talk about sex I was comfortable enough. I was sorry that I couldn't have been quick enough to point out to her the connection of her picking a fight with him the next morning after sex had been so positive.

Asking about debt counseling made me feel anxious that I would lose her as a client and that she isn't getting what she wants out of the sessions.

Plans for Future Action

To focus on figuring out with her what she really wants to get out of these meetings.

Questions

Since her presenting problem seemed to be how to handle her son, is it okay for me to be talking about money matters and sexual matters?

How do I help her continue our counseling sessions? She seems to want to see her problems in terms of money. At what point does this become a psychotherapy case that is beyond my skill?

Maddy brings this process recording to her field instruction meeting, and she and her field instructor review it together.

CASE ILLUSTRATION 6.2

JOINT FIELD INSTRUCTOR AND STUDENT REVIEW OF PROCESS RECORDING

Excerpt 1

Maddy's field instructor, Gilda, asked how she felt about the client's lateness that day. Maddy said she was relieved the client came to the session. The lateness made her feel anxious.

Her field instructor continued reading the process recording and then asked what Maddy felt about her client's issues with her son when she asked, "Why do you want your son to stop climbing?" and the client said, "To give me peace." Maddy stated that she felt annoyed and frustrated with the client because she doesn't seem to be connected to her child. Gilda asked what she might do to help the connection. Maddy suggested that she can ask Ms. Daniels to talk about her perceptions and observations of the child. Her field instructor encouraged this approach, noting, "This can help Ms. Daniels develop more empathy for her child and strengthen the attachment."

Her field instructor asked what Maddy felt when she told the client to "Relax." Maddy said she was feeling annoyed with the mother. "Do you think she does not know about child development, or is something else going on?" Maddy said she sees that Ms. Daniels is more focused on her marriage and is having a hard time

(Continued)

(Continued)

connecting to the child. Gilda asked, "How do you think she is feeling?" Maddy noted that she may be feeling alone or abandoned. Gilda asked, "What can you do to help her with that?" Maddy talked about how it must be hard to be with a toddler for most of the day and feel that your husband didn't want to come home and didn't care about your situation.

Discussion

Many teaching opportunities are provided in this process recording that allow the field instructor to support Maddy's learning and skill development. For one, it is apparent that Ms. Daniels is not fully attuned to her child. It is important to take note that Maddy has more work to do to understand her client. Ms. Daniels is not so well attuned to her husband, nor does her husband seem to show that he is attuned to his wife. The field instructor's main goal from reviewing this process recording would be to strengthen Maddy's empathic connection to her client. The field instructor will do this by being empathetic with Maddy.

Let's address another section in Maddy's process recording.

Excerpt 2

Ms. Daniels reported she had a good sexual experience with her husband the previous night and then argued with him over the train ticket he bought. Gilda asked what Maddy thought of this. She said she did not figure it out until later that Ms. Daniels was pushing her husband away. Gilda credited this observation and suggested she point that out to her client, noting another chance would present itself for her to make this observation. In reading the process recording further, where Ms. Daniels goes on to say that debt counseling might be better than counseling, Gilda asked Maddy how she felt after that comment. Maddy discussed becoming anxious that she would lose the client and angry that the client was back on the concrete issue of money. Gilda noted she probably makes her husband feel this way too. "Suggesting that you would refer her to debt counseling was a good strategy, and then saying you thought more was going on that she could work on kept her engaged. How did you feel at that point?" Maddy said she felt empowered and that she was starting to get a handle on the client. "I see how hard it is for her and how abandoned she must feel." Gilda suggested that Maddy stay with those feelings when she meets her next time.

Discussion

There is much more to be considered and reviewed in this session. For now, the field instructor's goal is to focus Maddy's attention on her empathic understanding of her client. For Maddy, the act of writing this process recording has created the opportunity for reflection that likely would not have come about without this document.

CASE ILLUSTRATION 6.3

FIRST-YEAR STUDENT—BOYS' GROUP MEETING FOR 10- AND 11-YEAR-OLDS

Pre-Engagement

I prepared to meet this group: Harris, Joe, Fred, Rocky, Lavaughn, Louie, Hector, and Damon. I am getting to know them. This is the fourth session. I did a game last week, and we went outside to play penny toss while the weather was still nice. Then we came back, and I had them do homework.

After my last group meeting, my field instructor suggested I have them talk about how school is going—what they like and what they do not like. In doing that, I will learn more about what they need.

Narrative

I started the group with some snacks that the center provides for the kids in the after-school program. Then I was about to start asking if someone wanted to tell us about something that went on in school today. Somehow they didn't stay with that question, and Harris started poking Fred. Fred eventually got up and changed his seat. I asked Harris why he was poking Fred. The other kids started laughing while I tried to explore more with Harris because he does this to kids who sit next to him.

The other kids in the group were not really paying attention. I decided to redirect by asking the group how school has been. I called on Fred to tell us what his day was like. Fred said that he went to school with his cousin Jenna who is older and goes with him. He likes Jenna because she brings him treats. Rocky jumped in and said that he has a very strict teacher but that the other kids in the class say they like her because she got them to work hard and learn things. I asked Rocky what he wants to learn. He said this year they are supposed to study ancient Greece, and he thinks all those Greek gods like Zeus and the Spartan fighters are great. He said he got a Spartan helmet. Damon piped in that he is mad because he was not put into a class with his friend Hector. Damon said he thinks they were split up because they both speak Spanish. Hector did not say anything. They went on talking about all the homework they have. Sometimes they talked at once.

I asked if any of them are in the same class. Damon and Fred are in class together. I wondered if Fred felt badly that Damon wanted to be with Hector. I didn't ask.

(Continued)

(Continued)

I gave them a stack of colored paper and markers and asked them to draw the perfect student. That was fun. Some of the boys put funny hats on the student— like the hat of a current pop star. Joe put on a baseball shirt. I know that he plays Little League with Lavaughn. Fred loaded the boy with books. Harris drew a funny kid with a wide open mouth and a tongue licking an ice cream cone. Of course, everyone laughed. Some kids made the faces light tan but not brown. I saw that but didn't know where to go with it. We got into a discussion of why this is the perfect student. Harris said because he gets a treat after he does his homework. Then some of them talked more about the qualities. Fred said his sister reads a lot and carries way too many books. "She is the perfect student, and I try to be like that." Joe drew a boy with glasses. Then he shaded them in to look like sunglasses. Hector commented that you don't need sunglasses in the classroom. Joe said they look "chill." Damon wanted to know why he has to look chill.

I realized that time was starting to run out and that I had to give them a chance to do some of their homework. I suggested we save our further discussion for the next meeting and they should spend some time on homework to make it easier for them when they got home today. That worked.

Impressions

I liked the meeting, but it was hard at the beginning because of Harris being silly. But then when we started talking about school I thought they were interested. I liked breaking up the session with the drawings.

Plans for Future Action

I want to find out more about their school triumphs and difficulties. I am not sure how to do that. I can't tell yet who likes or doesn't like each other. They seem to like to come to the group, though. The idea that they were placed in separate classes because they speak Spanish is something to think about. The African American kids' drawings of ideal students with light tan faces bother me a lot.

Questions

What do I do when Harris starts acting up? How do I keep them interested? How do I observe and recognize their conflicts and underlying feelings? What do I do with the diversity issues?

The student, Riley, brings the process recording to his field instruction meeting, where he and his field instructor review and discuss his session with the boys.

CASE ILLUSTRATION 6.4

JOINT FIELD INSTRUCTOR AND STUDENT REVIEW OF PROCESS RECORDING

Excerpt 1

The field instructor, Ingrid, asked Riley why he pursued the discussion with Harris about poking. Riley said he wanted to see if Harris could think about why he pokes others. She asked him if he could have done this differently. Riley suggested that he could have asked Fred how it made him feel. Ingrid noted that he would be staying stuck on the two boys by asking that of Fred. She asked Riley to consider what the group was doing while he was talking with Harris. Riley said that it did not register until later that they were laughing. Ingrid asked why he thought they were laughing. Riley said that he believes the boys think Harris's antics are funny and that he might be the comedian, especially given what happened later with his drawing. Ingrid agreed and then asked how Riley felt during this exchange. He said he felt frustrated.

She then went on to tell Riley that it is important to talk to the group when an incident like this happens, not so much to the individual. "You were trying to do individual counseling in the group, and it didn't go too far." She suggested that he ask them what they think when Harris pokes a member, and said, "In this way, you can involve the group and keep everyone connected to the process." She noted that scanning the group when things are happening will give him a better feel for what is going on for everyone: "Look from person to person." Riley said that this was a new concept for him to think about. Ingrid advised, "You are trying to develop their ability to talk to each other, so you have to keep facilitating that type of communication rather than just talking to one individual." Riley said that he hoped he could do this. Ingrid said, "You imagine now that it will be hard, but once you get going, you will see how it will flow more easily."

Ingrid then suggested he read the classroom text's initial chapter on group work.

Then they move on to discuss the question he asked them about school. "How did you feel at that point?" Riley said he felt relieved because they responded, and he got away from the previous exchange. Ingrid noted that this was a group-focused question and the boys connected to it. She asked him to what extent did the boys

(Continued)

(Continued)

talk to each other and pointed to a series of statements they had made about the ancient Greek curriculum and a strict teacher and about an older cousin who brings treats. Riley said, "Come to think of it, they didn't talk much to each other. They talked to me." "Yes," Ingrid said, "It is an early stage phenomenon. It is part of the group's development, and your role is to keep connecting them. How could you have done that?" Riley said he could have asked who everyone else goes to school with. She agreed that he was on the right track, thinking about connections. She asked, "What about the Spartans?" I could have said, "Is anyone else going to learn about ancient Greece this year?" Ingrid added, "Or what other topics are you going to be learning? In these various ways you are showing them how to use their listening and communication skills."

Ingrid asked him about his calling on Fred after he asked them how school had been. Riley said because it was quiet and "I was afraid no one would answer or the silliness would start." She asked how else he could have preempted the silliness. He wasn't sure. She suggested he reinforce with the group by repeating the question in a different way—for example, that he thinks they would all gain something from sharing with each other on this topic.

They went on to talk about how the boys shared some interesting situations—being with friends in the classroom or possible alienation in the classroom. Ingrid suggested that scratching the surface on these topics was okay for a fourth meeting but that he could bring up these subjects again, including taking notice of whether Damon and Fred were making a connection.

Ingrid asked Riley what he thought of the comment about being placed in separate classes because they spoke Spanish. He had no way of knowing its basis in reality. Perhaps the boys were known to speak Spanish to each other, which some teachers may find fault with. She suggested he bring it up if he had an opening but to generalize the issue of difference in ethnicity, race, or religion to involve all the kids. They talked about the depictions of the ideal student as light tan in their drawings rather than brown like some of them. She suggested he follow up when he had an opening, noting that at this early stage in the group's development this would give them permission to discuss their own differences. They talked about lighter skin as more desirable and that the group needed further levels of cohesion to be open about the topic.

Ingrid asked Riley about his own ethnic background. He said he is of Irish and French Canadian heritage. She asked how he thought the kids saw him. He said the kids see him as white. They talked about what the kids' origins might be, including two white kids. She suggested he do an exercise using a world map with them to trace and discuss their origins and that Riley include himself in the activity. She talked about her own Danish background, her yearly visits, and efforts at improving her Danish language skills.

Excerpt 2

Ingrid asked how Riley felt when he gave the boys the colored paper and asked them to draw. He said he was happy he had thought of that activity and that so much came from it. Ingrid agreed and thought breaking up the meeting with the activity kept them involved and added that he got a lot of information from the boys through these drawings, including their feelings about skin color. "I also got a better understanding of Harris." She added, "and his leadership. Look how clever he is. People probably don't get him."

They talked more about each of the boys and if he could see who connected to whom in the group and outside of the group.

Excerpt 3

In discussing Riley's questions in his process recording, Ingrid suggested that they would give him ample chances to ask about school-related issues in future sessions and as they moved further into the school year and encouraged him to listen to the boys as he had been doing already. She suggested that he trust his ability to hear what they were saying.

Ingrid suggested that he try to observe at future meetings who talks to whom and who talks after whom. She asked him to take note of comments members make that are not picked up by others to look for isolation. She asked what Riley could do when noticing this phenomenon. He said that he could highlight the comment by restating it and then asking them what they thought.

ADDITIONAL FORMATS FOR PROCESS RECORDING

There are other types of process recording outlines that have been developed by schools and agencies. Some will require the student to provide more dialogue than this suggested narrative outline. Direct quotes are important to include throughout the process recording because they provide information on the clients' personalities. However, the additional dimension of telling the story provides more data about the student's observations, feelings, and use of theory. Some alternative formats may not include a pre-engagement section focused on preparation, which is vital in strengthening the student's ability to connect with and to hold on to their clients (Shulman, 2011).

In addition to the format presented in this chapter, another commonly used format is the column format. (See Appendix A, Column Format for an example.)

Usually in the first column, the student provides dialogue. In the second column, the student shares feelings. In the third column, the student writes the intent of intervention. In the fourth column, the student provides theory. A fifth column is for the field instructor's comments and questions. The well-conceived column format includes a pre-engagement section as well as sections on impressions, plans for future action, and questions. This format tends to work better with advanced-level students because they are able to more systematically dissect a session. First-year and senior-year bachelor in social work (BSW) students do better utilizing a holistic approach that gives them the flexibility to tell the story as it unfolds. Field instructors may ask the student to utilize a particular format depending upon their educational assessments of the students. (See Appendix A for other common process recording formats.)

FURTHER EDUCATIONAL TOOLS

First-year and second-year master in social work (MSW) students as well as senior-year BSW students will be asked to interview clients and prepare an assessment that will be used by the agency in a variety of ways. Students' intake interviews usually follow a format provided by the agency. The student asks questions, while at the same time maintaining empathic connection and departing from the pre-scribed question format to ask for details. Following that format, the student will prepare a more formal assessment. Second-year students in clinical settings will prepare biopsychosocial assessments, which are far more comprehensive than an initial intake interview and will usually include a clinical diagnosis. These assess-ments will give the agency guidelines for determining which services to provide, the services and entitlements clients qualify for, the extent to which the agency is equipped to meet the client's need, or if further referral is needed.

Fundamental assessment involves providing a social diagnosis of the person in a situation with a problem. The student gathers relevant information about the person, learning his or her definition of the problem, while at the same time considering the person's context. For example, each member of a client family consisting of several intergenerational individuals has to be understood for their unique histories and needs. One or several members will have an immediate problem that will also impact the others. In some clinical settings, the person with the problem may be called the "Identified Patient." The client who experienced a major stroke will need admission to a rehabilitation center to regain verbal and motor functioning. This client will be impacted by the loss of functioning and having to adapt to the setting. The client's wife will require support. The client's adult son, his wife, and children will be impacted by the client's situation and the need to provide support to the mother. Financial, medical, and other uncertainties will create further stress upon the family system.

The student intern trying to discharge the patient to a rehabilitation facility will prepare a comprehensive assessment of the patient, which includes family and medical supports that will help the patient gain admission to a facility. A community center screening youngsters for a day camp program will use an assessment tool to guide the student's collection of relevant data. If the family is requesting financial assistance, the child's need and the family's identifying financial information may be gathered along with other educational and social factors of the family and child. Similarly, a senior center that provides meal deliveries to homebound clients will use an assessment format to validate eligibility.

In mental health settings, students will write biopsychosocial assessments that will include clinical diagnoses and extensive histories that are not required in most foundation field placements. The following is a sample outline for biopsychosocial assessment:

1. Identifying data

2. Culture, race, religion, class, and gender

3. Presenting problem

4. Personal and family history

5. Medical history

6. Legal history

7. Educational/vocational history as it relates to presenting problem

8. Mental health or social service treatment history

9. Current level of functioning

10. Diagnostic impressions (*Diagnostic and Statistical Manual of Mental Disorders* [*DSM–5*], 2013) and prognosis based on strengths and limitations

11. Treatment plan

Students in field placements will be given one or several intake or assessment formats to follow in interviews with clients. Various formats may be found in textbooks and websites of state mental health offices (New York State, 2014, n.d.).

SUMMARY

This chapter discussed the essential elements of process recording as an educational tool for field instruction that facilitates students' reflection of their practice. This tool helps develop their skills and allows them to better connect with their clients and themselves. A five-part outline was presented that takes the student through the progression from preparing for client engagement to a narrative, telling the story of the interaction, and guiding the student to develop action plans and pose questions for learning. Further information was provided in preparing intake forms, utilizing assessment tools, and writing biopsychosocial assessment formats.

Chapter 7 considers the role of the faculty field advisor and the student's and field instructor's relationship to the advisor.

Chapter 7

The Relationship Between Faculty Field Advisor and Student

INTRODUCTION

Your faculty field advisor is the person at the school with whom you maintain an ongoing relationship about your learning in field work. As the go-to person when you have questions or concerns, your faculty field advisor's role as a sounding board will guide you through this process. Steady communication with him or her throughout the duration of field work is the most effective approach for guiding, clarifying, and redirecting you before field work issues turn into crises. Your faculty field advisor will maintain a relationship with your field instructor; he or she can then help to mediate any issues between you and your field instructor and help you gain clarity and perspective regarding assignments, field instruction, process recordings, and evaluation. This position has various titles depending upon your school, including field liaison, field advisor, and others. This text will use the title "faculty field advisor."

This chapter discusses the faculty field advisor's role with the student and with the field instructor, the student's relationship with an advisor, and the student's part in sustaining this relationship.

FACULTY FIELD ADVISOR'S ROLES

Faculty field advisors contribute to students' field work experiences in many ways. They keep in contact with the field instructor to ensure students are learning and growing in their roles at the agency, mediate any issues between students and field instructors, assign field work grades, and serve as the face of the school to the agency. This section discusses these roles and others in detail.

Conferring and Meeting With the Field Instructor

After the field office at the school assigns a student's field placement, the faculty field advisor monitors this placement and maintains contact with the student's field instructor to review the student's progress, ensuring that the field work assignment provides opportunities for learning and competency attainment.

He or she will schedule a meeting with the student and his or her field instructor—usually at the agency or through enhanced real-time online communication—to review the student's progress toward meeting learning goals and acquiring skills. It provides an opportunity to determine strengths, review process recordings, and assess gaps and needs for further development. Feedback will be provided to the student with the goal of enhancing further learning.

Evaluating the Student's Learning Experience

By seeing the student at the agency, the faculty field advisor is also the school's representative to the agency in understanding the strengths, weaknesses, and constraints of the agency experience. The faculty field advisor will strive to broaden the learning experience according to the student's level, such as if a second-year student needs a concentration assignment, or a first-year, senior-year, or junior-year student needs more generic tasks. The need for additional group work, individual, or community assignments will be determined and considered throughout the field work experience.

Mediating the Relationship Between Student and Field Instructor

The student–field instructor relationship is complex. From time to time, there may be a communication gap between the student and field instructor requiring intervention and mediation by the faculty field advisor. The faculty field advisor is usually able to facilitate the communication in order to enhance the student's learning.

Some students may come to their field work with a false confidence in their own abilities and will not take necessary direction from their field instructors. Other times, field instructors may have unrealistic expectations of students that prevent them from providing the needed structure and input students need to develop skill. Another common problem arises when a student has only a narrow understanding of social work practice. This can result in the student avoiding the assignments he or she is given and causing tension with his or her field instructor.

The faculty field advisor gathers information and facilitates the field instructor's development of realistic expectations and viable learning structures. At the same time, the advisor provides feedback to the student about the learning goals of particular assignments. These actions strengthen the student–field instructor relationship.

Acting as a Sounding Board for Students

If and when a student has questions about the validity of an assignment as a learning experience, it is productive to raise the issue with the faculty field advisor. For example, a student may say, "I do not understand why I'm being asked to take a client to housing court. Isn't the attorney supposed to do that?" The advisor can help the student recognize aspects of his or her resistance that he or she may not see. For example, one reason for avoiding this experience may have to do with the student's inability to understand social work's broad scope. Along with the attorney's advocacy, the social worker provides emotional support and helps this client recognize habits that may contribute to her potential eviction from her home. Although the student may not plan to work in the court system, some future clients will likely be involved with the court, whether they are in recovery or have been domestic abuse victims. In discussing the issue with the faculty field advisor, the student may recognize that the fear of the unknown was behind the avoidance of this role. This discussion can prevent the student from presenting negative reactions to the field instructor and facilitate taking on a challenge.

Assigning Field Work Grades

The student's faculty field advisor usually assigns the field work grade. Field work is a course for which the student earns many credits. For the most part, the grade given is in agreement with the field instructor's evaluation. However, the final authority for providing a grade rests with the school's designee. In some schools, the grade given by the faculty field advisor includes the field director's signature.

Consulting With Field Instructor on Educational Issues

Field instructors will look to the faculty field advisor for assistance in developing meaningful assignments, providing feedback to the student, and furthering their own skills as field instructors. They also seek clarification about the school's curriculum to ensure educational criteria are being met.

Representing School to Agency

The faculty field advisor is seen as the school's direct representative to the agency. Field instructors may ask for further information about competency guidelines as developed by the Council on Social Work Education (CSWE) and other pertinent educational and practice resources the university can provide.

Faculty field advisors will meet with the agency's program directors, task supervisors, directors, interdisciplinary staff, and educational coordinators from time to time to represent the school's curriculum and requirements and to learn more about what the agency may need from the school.

ROLES OF STUDENTS

While the roles that your faculty field advisor plays in your learning are important, the ways that you, as the student, utilize his or her help to grow and develop your skills is equally important. In order to do so, you have responsibilities as well, including being open to suggestions and learning new things, accurate reporting, and using your faculty field advisor as a sounding board.

Utilizing the Faculty Field Advisor's Resources

Every student in a school of social work will have a faculty academic advisor, and, if assigned to field work, a faculty field advisor. In many schools, the same person carries both roles. Your relationship with your faculty field advisor is an important part of your education and how proactive you are in utilizing the faculty member's resources may impact your field work experience.

Some students do not feel a great need to sustain their advisory relationship. They may believe that their field work is progressing well, and they do not need further advisement. It is important to test out that principle by meeting with your faculty field advisor to obtain his or her input regarding what more you could be doing and to consider your blind spots. Students who are progressing appropriately in field work can benefit from extra support to help increase their learning. Faculty field advisors may also be able to provide the student with additional understanding of the agency in its community context and help the student integrate field work and classroom content. A solid relationship with a faculty field advisor will offer unexpected rewards and outcomes.

Your faculty field advisor can help you to consider concentration options for second year. While they are not usually responsible for making field assignments, they are in a good position to guide you toward sound options for the future. Faculty field advisors can be helpful in directing second-year students and bachelor in social work (BSW) seniors toward future opportunities.

Students tend to rely on their field instructor for direction. However, the faculty field advisor usually has additional perspective on your overall performance and integration of theory with practice that can provide guidance for the next year—whether for another field placement or employment.

Benefiting From the Faculty Field Advisor's Agency Visit

The most effective use of the three-way meeting with the faculty field advisor, student, and field instructor onsite at the agency requires a major contribution from the student.

When your faculty field advisor visits your field placement site for the first time, you will serve as host. Make a plan ahead of time with your field instructor on the best approach to showing your faculty field advisor around the agency. Find out if you should do this or if it will be taken care of by your field instructor. Consider the time frame for the visit. The agency tour will generally be brief but necessary and useful for your faculty field advisor and agency. You must utilize your social skills to provide introductions and become a small-scale tour guide. Since the advisor is viewed by the agency as the school's representative, his or her site visit will be important to the agency. The field instructor may want to introduce your faculty field advisor to the executive director and/or program director, as well as to the educational coordinator. It will serve your advisor well if you prepare him or her ahead of time with information about the agency staff.

Your role as a student at this meeting is to follow the lead of your faculty field advisor and field instructor. You should prepare for this meeting in several ways. Start by thinking about what skills, perspectives, and self-awareness you have developed up until now. You should reflect on your new understanding of service delivery for the agency population. Then, consider the practice challenges or difficulties you have encountered and how you are working on these areas. Identify future learning goals and assignments as you continue in this field setting. Finally, think about how you and your field instructor are working together to enhance your learning.

Your faculty field advisor might begin the meeting by asking you to describe your assignments and learning. He or she will be curious to hear what classroom theories you have used to inform your work with clients. Your advisor will ask about your self-awareness issues—which clients stir up particular feelings or might be presenting a value conflict for you.

The anticipation of this meeting may make you anxious. Whether or not your field work has been smooth, do your best to bring an open perspective that indicates your willingness to listen and learn. Your faculty field advisor wants you to succeed and grow in your professional development. You will have to do your part to accept feedback.

CASE ILLUSTRATION 7.1

FACULTY FIELD ADVISOR WITH SECOND-YEAR CLINICAL STUDENT

Phil is a 35-year-old second-year student in a clinical concentration. He has the reputation of being a very good student—in class and in field—to the extent that other students look to him for guidance. His first-year field placement in substance abuse treatment gave him an opportunity to do long-term clinical work with adults. His second-year placement is in a mental health clinic. His field instructor has been having difficulty identifying adult clients for Phil due to insurance constraints. However, they have increased his caseload by giving him several children. He had not asked to work with children and initially felt he did not have an affinity to them and does not have children himself.

At the three-way meeting, his field advisor asked him to talk about how he feels his work with the children has been progressing. Phil spoke openly about his initial reluctance in learning to communicate with children and of his decision to take a course on practice with children and adolescents. He discussed using play techniques he learned in class and even taking one of the kids out for ice cream on several occasions to build the relationship and the child's feelings of being nurtured. He developed the patience to find out a great deal from his clients.

His field instructor suggested he tell his advisor about his countertransference issues as they came up with the kids. Phil talked about his father's rigidities and how dealing with the children brought some of his issues to the surface again. He found himself initially urging the kids to "do the right thing," by focusing on their academics. He was copying his father's parenting style. By learning to explore their issues, he developed a better understanding of how to support the children's strengths and desires. His advisor supported his self-reflection. Phil was honest in saying that he was initially resistant to this exploration. He identified with one child who wanted to pursue music because he himself had been an animation artist.

His field instructor noted Phil's disappointment in not having more adult clients. He saw three clients and ran two groups in the day program. This assignment had whetted his desire to work with persons with serious mental illness.

Phil has seen so much progress in several of his clients that he wants to do the best he can before leaving them when field work ends. His goals are to use focusing skills better and to help his clients build self-esteem—the adults stigmatized by mental illness and the vulnerable children who need to see a positive future. He plans to develop their social and communication skills.

Discussion

At this meeting, Phil was able to show he learned from the experience, that he was adaptable and flexible, and used the placement well, despite its drawbacks and imperfections. Phil demonstrated openness and honesty in the meeting and handled himself nondefensively.

CASE ILLUSTRATION 7.2

FIRST-YEAR STUDENT IN SENIOR CENTER WITH MANY CHINESE MEMBERS

Ted is a first-year student placed in a senior center with many Cantonese-speaking members. He is having a great deal of difficulty in his social interactions. Despite speaking Cantonese, he is unable to walk around the center making connections and engaging with the seniors. In his group interaction, his process recordings have shown anxiety and frozen behavior. This is corroborated by the seniors who gave feedback to the director about his lack of connection.

The faculty field advisor visited the agency after five weeks. In the three-way meeting, Ted had difficulty receiving the feedback. In one group, he was supposed to have a discussion of the day's news events by going over the newspaper headlines. He was unable to read the paper in English or say much to the group in Cantonese. His faculty field advisor asked Ted to tell them what he thinks happened at that meeting. It becomes evident that Ted is always trying to consider what kinds of "interventions" to make. He focuses on what he should say rather than listening to what is being said. He also does not show skills of exploration. As a result, he does not connect with either the client or the group. Lack of connection does not reduce his anxiety: It fuels his anxiety. His faculty field advisor pointed this out to him in this meeting. Ted then discussed his own psychotherapy and his attempts to cope with his chronic anxiety.

The decision is made that Ted should not remain at the senior center. The demands for high levels of formal and informal interaction are far too difficult for him to overcome. A further decision is made to find another placement for him and to put him on probation with an eight-week plan.

Accurately Reporting Events to the Faculty Field Advisor

A vital part of your experience in your practice with clients is determining how to report the goings-on between you and clients so that you can obtain feedback to develop skills. One set of skills includes the accurate reporting of client data in professional assessments and other materials. This skill set is an ethical imperative.

You will also have to develop the skills of accurately reporting what goes on in your role as a social work student. This involves describing an interaction to your field instructor even when it does not present you in a positive light. It is important that you report the same information to all parties. Changing the events for different people is not professional. Bending the facts to your advantage not only harms you but it harms your client. It also causes others to question your credibility. Therefore, it is important that you represent events with minimal bias.

CASE ILLUSTRATION 7.3

PANIC-STRICKEN FIRST-YEAR STUDENT

The student has been feeling her field instructor has not spent the required amount of time supervising her recently. She brought this issue to her faculty field advisor and said, "My field instructor has not met with me for one month." When her advisor asked for specifics, the student said that she had a crisis with a client and could not locate the field instructor. The field advisor contacted the field instructor only to discover that the student had canceled the last two field instruction sessions due to a health problem. The field instructor also told the faculty field advisor that the student was panic stricken when she could not find the field instructor who had appointments at that time. The student also knew to use the clinical director in the event of an emergency if the field instructor was unavailable.

By omitting essential facts, the student placed her faculty field advisor in the uncomfortable situation of trying to advocate for her when there was no reason to do so. This drew her field instructor into an unwarranted potential conflict with the agency field instructor.

The faculty field advisor brought this discrepancy to the student, who ultimately admitted that she had canceled the meetings due to a health problem. Much drama would have been avoided had the student not tried to blame the field instructor for her own shortcomings. With these actions, the student presented herself in a less than credible manner that had far worse implications than the error made in cancel-ing her field instruction sessions. The lessons of this story are as follows: Panic will ensue if you cancel your field instruction sessions. Trying to place blame on others will always come back to you.

CASE ILLUSTRATION 7.4

FIELD INSTRUCTOR LEAVING AGENCY

The field instructor informed the student that she might be leaving the agency one month before field work ends. The student brought this information to his faculty field advisor, who requested further details. The student is concerned about receiv-ing an evaluation before the field instructor's departure and is anxious about the possibility of not having supervision. He is also somewhat angry because he wants his field instructor to stay to the end of his experience. However, agency funding is being cut and the field instructor needed to ensure continued employment, which is why she is leaving.

The student and his faculty field advisor decided that the field advisor would contact the field instructor to find out if the agency knows about her intent to leave and to find out what plans are being made for the student's supervision through the ending process. The faculty field advisor hopes the agency will allow the field instructor to continue to meet with the student for the last month of field work. If the agency does not approve this arrangement, the advisor will ask the agency to locate an interim field instructor.

The student agreed that although this is not an ideal situation, he has had a very positive experience and does not want to overreact to this glitch at the end.

Discussion

The student's reporting to his faculty field advisor was accurate. The advisor's request for more details presented additional information that helped them to plan the advisor's contact with the field instructor. The faculty field advisor told the field instructor that she knew about her imminent departure and assured her she would give her time to tell the agency. Once the field instructor informed the agency, they came up with two possibilities for having the student end the year. How the student handled the information from his field instructor posed no credibility gap. He did not escalate the situation by saying that he was being abandoned and uncared for.

Using the Faculty Field Advisor as a Sounding Board

Field work is messy, and much of what occurs cannot be tied up into neat packages, so to speak. Agency occurrences will undoubtedly raise many questions for a student to consider. The student's faculty field advisor will have a knowledgeable point of view about the agency. He or she is the one to whom these issues should be brought.

The following illustration shows concerns regarding treatment approaches with clients.

The following example shows boundary and role issues that the student should not be involved in.

CASE ILLUSTRATION 7.5

STUDENT AT SENIOR CENTER WORKING WITH CLIENT WHO HOARDS

An elderly homebound client with a history of hoarding has been encouraged to use the agency van system at least once a week to visit the senior center. She recently told Leila, a first-year student, that she does not like the people who go to the center. Leila feels she should continue to see the client at home. When she raised this issue with her field instructor, the answer she received did not fully satisfy her. The field instructor said that it is good for the client to try to leave home, even if she does not like the people at the center. She told Leila that she is being overprotective of the client and urged her to work with the client to take a risk and come to the center once a week.

Leila was annoyed that her field instructor was not sympathetic enough of the client, and she raised this concern with her faculty field advisor, Dr. Atkin. Dr. Atkin agreed with her field instructor and asked Leila to consider if she is being too protective of her client. This discussion saved Leila from getting into conflict with her field instructor who told her the same thing—but she did not want to hear it.

CASE ILLUSTRATION 7.6

STUDENT BECOMES INVOLVED IN A SITUATION THAT IS NOT HER BUSINESS

Wendy is ambivalent about her field placement and told her faculty field advisor, Dr. Holmes, that students at her placement from other schools have been complaining because they receive only group and not individual supervision. Wendy then told Dr. Holmes that the agency is "unprofessional."

Her faculty field advisor discussed these perceptions with Wendy, helping her to understand her student role and the boundary issues involved. The boundary issue in this incident is about her role as a student. Dr. Holmes recommended that Wendy tells her colleagues to bring the issue to their faculty field advisors if they are unhappy about their field instruction. While she may be troubled by this and cares about her colleagues, Wendy's primary role is to focus on her own learning and relationship with her field instructor. Her faculty field advisor also suggested that the other school might use an educational design involving group supervision as the primary modality. Wendy has difficulty accepting these ideas.

In their follow-up meeting, Dr. Holmes asked how Wendy is working with her field instructor and if she suggested to her peers that they bring their issue to their own advisors.

Dr. Holmes told Wendy that in this "teaching moment," she wanted her to know that the term *unprofessional* should not be used without reflection. She noted that students have the same responsibility as professionals to weigh their words. Part of learning is to follow the NASW (National Association of Social Workers) *Code of Ethics* (NASW, 2008). Calling someone unprofessional is a serious accusation that requires prudence. It is best for a student to be descriptive about behavior rather than accusatory. Wendy thanked her and said she will think about this.

SUMMARY

This chapter highlighted the relationship between the student and faculty field advisor. It presented elements of the field advisor's role that contribute greatly to the student's field work experience, such as assessing a student's learning, mediating the student–field instructor relationship, and serving as a sounding board for the student. Also discussed were the roles that students must play to get the most out of their field work experience. These included the student as a proactive participant in the student–field instructor–faculty field advisor meeting, the necessity for accurate reporting, accepting feedback, and utilizing the advisor's resources.

Chapter 8 begins Part III: Transforming the Desire to Help Into Professional Skill. The chapter provides a field work timeline and tools for embracing the role of student.

Transforming the Desire to Help into Professional Competence: From Caring to Learning How to Do

Chapter 8

Timelines for Student Development

INTRODUCTION

Many students need an orientation on how to use classroom learning and field education to conduct themselves with clients. Some students require more explanation and analysis of experiential education concepts than others. Those who are apprehensive about applying theory to each unique client situation may wish for prescriptive answers.

This chapter is designed to help you integrate theory with the realities of the client. A timeline is included to guide you through those challenging learning-how-to-learn endeavors.

BSW PROGRAM FIELD WORK TIMELINE

Starting the field work experience in a bachelor in social work (BSW) program can seem daunting due to what you feel to be a lack of experience. However, the field work timeline consists of three phases that will help to cultivate your competencies.

Beginning Phase of Field Work: Junior-Year and Senior-Year Students in the First Semester

The learning issues for baccalaureate students are parallel to those of first-year master's students. Acquiring a beginning framework to understand the social work role started in the junior-year field placement. Thus, you were able to enter a senior-year placement with familiarity. However, you will be given tasks to complete and directions to follow from your field instructor about reviewing a client's file and following up by using engagement skills. Some of what you will be asked to do will build on your junior-year experience, and some actions will be completely new.

During the first semester of senior year, you will have to follow directions from your field instructor despite not understanding the reasons behind these directions. You may expect to conduct more informal interactions with clients only to be told that maintaining professional boundaries is required. More evidence and understanding will be presented in your coursework to guide your development as a social worker.

By the end of the first half of senior year, you should be able to integrate classroom theory with practice at your agency. Practice papers written during the first senior semester will focus on applying theory to your client's situation. At this time, seniors should know what the social worker's role entails. Some students may be having difficulty in the task of integrating theory with practice. Reading more not only from your texts but from relevant journal articles will help you proceed effectively. You should begin the second half of senior-year field work at Stage 3 (in the stage model of education): Knowing What You Have to Do But Not Always Being Able to Do It (Reynolds, 1942).

Middle and Ending Phases of Field Work: Senior-Year Student in the Second Semester

During the second half of senior-year field placement, you will continue to develop foundation skills and competencies. You will strengthen your ability to practice with clients and build engagement, assessment, intervention, and evaluation skills in all settings through the use of classroom discussions. By the end of senior year, you should have developed social work competencies at the foundation level. (Chapter 9 discusses foundation competencies in depth.) As a senior, you will reflect on the foundation competencies you have attained so that you may earn your BSW degree and plan for your future, whether it involves finding a job, applying to a master in social work (MSW) program, or going on to something else. It will be helpful to review the Council on Social Work Education (CSWE) list of competencies (Chapter 4) by focusing on the assessment of your competencies in your field evaluations and feedback from your foundation practice instructor and field advisor.

In some instances, students may not demonstrate sufficient competency attainment. They may be asked to extend field work or to repeat field work. A faculty review committee may become involved in assessing the student's competency attainment as well as overall professionalism. This review will usually result in the development of an educational plan to help the student achieve his or her learning goals.

Utilizing your faculty field advisor's expertise to enhance planning and future directions is critical. He or she can help you to take stock of your skills and accomplishments and focus on moving forward effectively.

MSW PROGRAM TIMELINE FOR FIELD WORK

Uncertainty and anxiety may be how you begin your field work experience, but it will not be how you end this process. There are three phases in the process that will allow your knowledge and skills to build and grow.

Beginning Phase of Field Work: First-Year Student in the First Half

During the first semester of a four-semester MSW program, you will have to embrace the uncertainties of not knowing exactly what you are doing. At your newly assigned field placement, your field instructor will direct you on how to read a client file, how to meet your clients at the outset, and how the agency's scope of practice defines how you present your purpose to clients. Some actions will be clarified in your classroom literature. Some information about the clients' psychosocial issues will be unfamiliar.

It will take your first semester to understand most of what you are doing. During this time, you will have to trust your field instructor's guidance and follow what you are asked to do with a client. If you have been employed in social services, you will already have some knowledge. However, you will encounter various practice approaches with clients who are unfamiliar or may contradict what you have been doing. These new practice perspectives will require you to adjust your mind-set and your practices.

Typically, by the end of your first semester of field work and its partner practice courses, you will understand the role of the social worker. At this time, you will have a good grasp of what you should be doing with your clients. Classroom discussion among peers in other field work settings and your written work will highlight the application of social work skill across populations and where your agency's services fall within the broader scope of the profession.

Middle Phase of Field Work: First-Year Student in the Second Half

The second half of your first year of MSW field work will be spent developing and broadening your social work skills. In the stage model of education (Reynolds, 1942), you will continue in Stage 3: Knowing What You Have to Do But Not Always Being Able to Do It. You will experience the joy of doing something really well and the discomforts of being incapable or awkward. By the end of the first year, you should have developed social work competencies at the foundation level. These identified competencies and expectations are found in your school's curricular guidelines and will be highlighted as criteria for student performance in first-year field work. Chapter 9 discusses competency attainment in depth.

In instances where a student may not demonstrate sufficient competency attainment, he or she may be asked to extend field work or to repeat field work. A faculty review committee will usually assess the student's competency attainment and overall professionalism. This review will provide an educational plan to help the student achieve his or her learning goals.

Middle Phase of Field Work: Second-Year Specialization

The middle phase of social work field education continues throughout your second year. Your second-year area of specialization is designed to deepen social work competencies in a particular area in a school's curriculum. Schools' second-year specializations tend to focus on social problem areas such as poverty or violence or on fields of practice such as children and families, child welfare, mental health, health and disabilities, and alcohol and substance abuse treatment. Other curricula may include methods based on clinical practice with individuals and families, clinical practice with groups, community social work, and social policy planning and administration. Chapters 9 and 10 describe the competencies to be attained in the foundation year and those to be attained in the second year of specialization.

Immediately upon starting the second year, you will apply what you learned in first year to the current setting. The second-year setting will be different in some aspects. Although it is tempting to enter second year with an attitude of self-protecting innocence, you must begin the placement by examining what you learned in first year about the beginning phase of practice and carrying this knowledge into second year. This includes skills of engagement and the ability to develop a studied assessment. Do not fake lack of knowledge or skill.

Consider what you know how to do. As a second-year student, you will learn the specific knowledge base that guides practice in your area of specialization. For example, in first year you learned how to engage clients in a senior center. Now you are in a fast-paced medical setting where you will have to engage quickly. You will scramble to gather relevant information and use what is necessary for your purpose. Or, if you are working with mandated clients, you will have to engage more resistant or unwelcoming clients. Perhaps in your BSW program, you were not required to diagnose clients using the *Diagnostic and Statistical Manual of*

Mental Disorders (DSM–5; 2013). However, in your second-year mental health setting, you will start using this material on your first day.

Throughout the second year, you will build on the skills and competencies that you acquired in your first year. For instance, suppose your specialization is group work. Your assessment will focus on group dynamics, including group norms, leadership, authority issues, and interventions in varied groups. In addition, you will learn how to assess individuals within the group. This is subtle and sophisticated learning that increases what you already know about assessing individuals, families, communities, and groups.

If your concentration is poverty, your practice interventions in a homeless families' shelter will focus on improving their current living conditions as well as future life chances. Assessments will focus on family structure, dynamics, and resources, along with the family's interaction with social institutional factors. Short-term interventions will be planned that maximize the family's economic resources such as employment and housing, members' educational supports, and mental health needs. Skills to enhance the long-range goals that move them out of poverty will be developed. What you learned in first-year placement with children and parents in a Head Start program will serve as your foundation. Though your previous clients were economically vulnerable, they did not experience crises associated with homelessness. Therefore, the skills and competencies you develop in a second-year specialization will be more focused on addressing impoverished resources.

Your participation in field instruction must be more sophisticated and proactive in the second year. Your considerations of your skill and self-awareness reflections will require more depth. Your own countertransference issues will require recognition in clinical work and in policy and administration as well. It is necessary to recognize that countertransference applies across all specializations and is not confined to clinical practice. Your relationships with clinical clients and stakeholders will be impacted by your reactions to them, at times helping and at times hindering your work. The affects accompanying power and authority in community practice will highlight your own issues with authority or as an authority figure (Shulman, 2011). This understanding is vital in your role as an ethical social worker providing fair services. This ethical imperative provides the foundation for being able to access supervision after completing the MSW degree.

Students who are not functioning at the required level of competency are given feedback by their field instructors, faculty field advisors, and directors of field instruction at their school about how to improve the work in order to meet requirements for competency attainment. When a student is found not to be meeting requirements, he or she will usually have great difficulty overcoming the hurt, anger, and disappointment experienced at being informed he or she is not passing field work. Although this crisis situation is usually very painful, it is important to endeavor to listen to the feedback you are being given rather than to focus on the painful feelings or the narcissistic blow that often comes with being informed you are not meeting requirements. Most often, the schools' faculty will have carved out a pathway to help you achieve future success beyond the stumbling blocks. This may involve repeating field work, or taking a leave of absence in order to deal with particular emotional and/or academic impediments obstructing your progress. Students who are able to accept the feedback and follow the path created for them by the school's educators are usually able to graduate and attain their goals for future success in social work.

CHALLENGES FOR ALL STUDENTS

During the beginning phase of learning social work practice, the student who needs to understand before doing faces a major challenge. Everyone requires some understanding before jumping into action. If you find you are not taking a speedy leap into the task, reflect upon whether you are asking for too much understanding. In the final analysis, you will have to suspend judgments and trust the directions you are being given.

CASE ILLUSTRATION 8.1

FIRST-YEAR STUDENT—TRUSTING A FIELD INSTRUCTOR'S DIRECTION

First-year student Eleanor recently began working with an elderly client at a nursing home who lost her husband to a car accident 35 years ago. During her last session, the client talked about how happy she was to attend her grandson's wedding. She noted that her son was able to be there whereas his own father had died before his wedding. She said her son did not discuss this with her at the wedding, but she believed he had considered the parallel.

Eleanor asked if she had brought this up to her son. She did not, saying that he does not like it when she talks about his father.

She never married her longtime boyfriend (who died recently) because she did not want to be disloyal to her husband or to betray her children. This puzzled Eleanor, but she did not say more.

In meeting her field instructor, Kate, Eleanor wanted to know how to talk with her client about why she does not discuss her late husband with her son. Kate told her not to raise that topic, telling her this is a long-standing issue with her son. The client worries her son will die young and passing the milestone of the grandson's wedding has given her comfort. Kate told Eleanor that it is a good sign that she did not bring this up to her son and is learning not to impose her anxieties onto him.

Kate wants Eleanor to affirm the positive relationship with the client's son, grandson, and her other son. If she discusses the parallels, it is important for Eleanor to ask what the client is feeling and to keep her focused on building the relationships with those who are living.

Discussion

Eleanor has to act upon what her field instructor is asking and accept that this client's relationship with her son is in delicate balance. Eleanor still wants to explore the client's feelings of loss. However, social work practice is complex. In this case, practice involves understanding family dynamics and how different family members cope with loss. Not allowing a family member to die is one issue that recurs, especially when someone dies young. The death of a young father may hover over a family, often due to the persistence of one member, and pervade the life force of the others. This persistence usually requires redirection. At this time, Eleanor does not know enough about these dynamics and practice perspectives. Thus, she is required to trust her field instructor's direction. After further sessions with the client, additional supervision, and subsequent classwork, Eleanor will gain clarity in these perspectives.

PROGRESSION OF LEARNING

When you are new to the field work experience—or if you are experienced but have moments of uncertainty—you may feel like you'll never understand or have the skills that you need to be successful in working with clients. Do not be discouraged—you will get there. The case illustrations in this section demonstrate the process and time it takes to feel competent and confident in your role.

Developing Higher-Order Understanding and Skills

Recall the case illustration from Chapter 6 regarding the first-year student, Riley, who was working with a group of 10- and 11-year-old boys. At the beginning of the session, one of the boys, Harris, began poking another boy, Fred. Riley focused on a discussion with Harris about poking, and in his review with his field instructor, Ingrid, she spoke to him about the importance of speaking with the group about the incident, rather than the individual. Though Riley was unaware of this practice, it proved to be a good learning opportunity, particularly because he was open to Ingrid's guidance. Like Riley, over time, your learning opportunities will expand your knowledge and you will gain enough understanding to guide and direct your practice. This learning progression is illustrated in the continuation of Riley's journey.

CASE ILLUSTRATION 8.2

BSW SENIOR-YEAR STUDENT IN THE SECOND SEMESTER— BOYS' GROUP COHESION

The group has been moving along, and Riley has been working with the boys to high-light behaviors that help them succeed in school and in their friendships. Harris continued as the group comedian. The group's cohesion has allowed the students to develop a writing project in which they created several short comedy skits about daily situations they would like to make fun of. This project strengthened the group's bond. They made fun of texting. They made fun of boys trying to look cool. They made fun of each other.

They had several talks about their different racial and ethnic identities, and the input Riley received from his field instructor framed their discussions. They have scratched the surface in talking about skin color but they used the world geography session with a map to trace their own ethnic, racial, and religious identities.

Making fun of everything opened the door for Riley to ask if there were serious things they wanted to bring up.

A couple of boys talked about hard things at home. Joe's older brother went to Afghanistan, and this makes him cry. Riley was especially pleased to see how kind Harris was to Joe, who told him to "come to my house" when he misses his brother. Ingrid praised Riley's question to the group as a whole and how much they have opened up.

Riley has come to understand why dealing with Harris's poking was not going to be helpful. Humor was his way of reaching out. Turning humor and the need for connection into something creative led to a cohesion that facilitated talk about further issues.

Riley is sad to end with this group right before graduation. An ending party will be held; pictures will be taken of all the members. Everyone will have mementos, including a scrapbook they have been working on to show the next worker.

Riley has earned his BSW and accepted a job in a different agency with teens. He has decided to apply to MSW programs for the following year.

CASE ILLUSTRATION 8.3

MSW SECOND-YEAR STUDENT IN THE FIRST SEMESTER— BOYS' GROUP

Riley, the senior BSW student facilitating the boys' group, terminated with the kids and graduated. Dan's second-year field placement in a children and families specialization includes working with this same group in the after-school program. In his first year, Dan learned not to do individual counseling in a group, so he will start off at a more advanced level than Riley. Dan has been reflecting on how he will enter an already-formed group.

Dan began the session by telling the boys a little bit about being a second-year student at his school and that he is specializing in kids and families. He then asked them to introduce themselves and to share what the group has been doing all year. He asked for some highlights of what has gone on. Although his field instructor, Ingrid, has given him information, obtaining it from the boys will be different. They showed Dan their album and told him what they had been doing until Riley ended with them. Dan encouraged them to describe their skits and Harris and the others gave more information. One boy noted that Dan is a student like Riley. Another asked when he was going to leave. Dan was taken aback and said it will be in May—that he will end with them near the time when their school ends. Dan was not sure how they were reacting, but decided to go on getting more of the group's history.

Dan told them he found their skits smart and fun and asked if they would like to show him a skit or two. He was so pleased with their excitement about their group and how active they became in figuring out how to demonstrate the vignettes. Harris poked a couple of kids to volunteer. Hector and Frank took part with Harris directing.

After a couple of skits were shown about being cool versus being real, Dan asked what they would like to do in the future. They talked more about skits, and Dan saw that serious material did not come up. He affirmed their ideas and told them he was excited to get to know them and thanked them for telling him so much already. They seemed to be winding down, and Dan asked if there was more they wanted to bring up. They said no, and he encouraged them to look at their homework.

(Continued)

(Continued)

Dan shared his impressions of the group with his field instructor, Ingrid, telling her that they felt cohesive and well organized. She asked about their leadership structure. It appeared that Harris and Fred talked more to Dan than the others and Harris seemed to be the group spokesman. She asked why he stayed with the funny topics, and Dan said he did not want to push them yet to talk about more difficult topics since they were also feeling him out. She added that feeling him out includes wondering how he will handle serious topics. Dan reflected that he did not communicate that so clearly.

Dan talked about taking over someone else's group and wondered if the kids will connect with him as much as they did with Riley. Ingrid liked that Dan framed his departure to coincide with the end of school.

Dan agreed he would let them know that serious topics are important and that he would find out which issues they had dealt with this past year. Ingrid also suggested he ask what Riley had done that they liked so that he could try to incorporate some of those things—but also making it clear that he and Riley are different people. She noted that the purpose of this is to develop the boys' skills in understanding how the behaviors of grown-ups impact them and to deal more openly with whatever comparisons they are making.

Discussion

Dan entered second-year field work knowing what a group should look like and how to engage the group members in talking about themselves and the group as a whole. His comments show that he knows that counseling an individual in the group is not the most effective way to proceed. He also shows recognition of the group's progress as a cohesive entity whose members can handle more challenging issues. His task for the future is to find ways of helping members function in depth with each other. Dan uses his field instructor well and is attentive to her suggestions and feedback.

Continuing to Develop Competencies

Dan's skill development is building now. As a second-year fourth semester student, Dan has also been incorporating diagnostic content relevant to the boys in his group. He is expanding his understanding by applying family dynamics theory to gain clarity about the impact the family has on each of the boys.

CASE ILLUSTRATION 8.4

MSW SECOND-YEAR STUDENT IN THE SECOND SEMESTER— BOYS' GROUP ENDING

In his four months of work with the boys group, Dan appreciated the meaning of mutual aid and how members helped each other deal with scary and difficult concerns. Louie, Fred, and Joe lifted each other up as they handled their losses while also gaining support from the group. Joe's brother was still in the military; Fred's mother has been ill and he has been living with his grandmother. Louie has a disabled younger sibling whom the family pays a lot of attention to. Dan encouraged the members to support each other even when the issues are not similar to their own. This boosted their confidence in their empathic abilities.

Rocky and Lavaughn were both diagnosed with attention deficit/hyperactivity disorder (ADHD), and recently they talked about it in the group. Harris and Joe were especially concerned, and when either Rocky or Lavaughn faded into the distance, one of them would bring him back—with Harris often doing his usual poke. When the poke didn't work, he would stick his face under Lavaughn's nose, which invariably brought him back and caused a laugh. During homework time, Joe was especially attentive to Lavaughn and Rocky.

Through this process, Dan began to look at relevant diagnostic issues, including ADHD, the cognitive impairment of Louie's brother, the withdrawn qualities of Hector, and the behavior disorder of Damon. Learning about these conditions deepened Dan's understanding of the group's current direction and how the group was being used to develop the boys' abilities and affects, while at the same time helping them channel and contain their behavior.

As the end of the school year approaches, it becomes apparent that not only will Dan be leaving but the group itself will not continue. The boys will be going to various schools and no longer coming to the center. The group planned a closing event of activities and a cookout at a campsite. Pictures were taken; contact information was exchanged. The boys expressed sadness about ending and were sad to terminate with Dan as well. In all his client work, this ending was the hardest and the most gratifying.

Dan graduated with an MSW degree. He passed the licensing exam and secured a job in a mental health program servicing urban high school youth.

BLOCK PLACEMENT TIMELINES

Block placements are usually field assignments carried out by the student without taking concurrent coursework. Courses are usually taken before block field placements begin. Block placements may be more intense because the time frame is shortened, with students completing many hours in a briefer amount of time. Although more accelerated, beginning, middle, and ending phases will follow the same progression as a traditional field placement. In the block placement timeline, the student must put forth special effort to make earlier classroom learning relevant to the field placement. Reviewing notes and literature from courses helps the student apply theory appropriately with clients. If you have a block field placement, you will do best by developing a consistent strategy for applying theory while moving through the field placement.

Schools with block placements should have structures that provide supports for integrating theory with practice. Some schools may require students to submit weekly logs to their faculty field advisors during a block placement. Log formats usually require application of theory. This mandates that students revisit their books to integrate theory into their everyday functioning with clients. In field instruction meetings, students will have to apply theory appropriately to the practice situation presented to them. A common pitfall for block placement students is to become overly dependent on the field instructor for guiding their application of theory.

Second-year block placements are designed so that students can complete field work in their specialization areas. They will have to draw from coursework to support the development of advanced-level skills in their specialization.

All support structures will have to be used, and students should demonstrate proactive application of theory to their practice situation as it is relevant to their specialization. The competencies that students will have to acquire by the end of a senior-year, first-year, or second-year block field placement are the same as those for students in concurrent placements.

SUMMARY

This chapter presented a series of timelines to guide students in moving through field work at the senior-year BSW level, the first-year MSW level, and the second-year MSW level. It described the beginning, middle, and ending stages of each level of field placement. It illustrated differences in learning at the three levels and focused on how students might approach developing skills and competencies for each. This process takes time, but students' skills increase with each level. Finally, when faced with potential challenges because of inexperience, students should consider their client's qualities, including background, age, needs, and so on, as well as their own appearance and presentation, which can affect their client's opinion of them.

Chapter 9 describes the process of competency attainment in the foundation year.

Chapter 9

Developing Social Work Competencies in the Foundation Year

INTRODUCTION

Students face ongoing challenges in trying to develop skills while doing the right thing for clients. They may be confused about how to use a skill or are uncertain about what exactly is the "right thing." Students have to develop a skill set and social work competencies. But they have to do this in the minute by minute affective exchange with clients. Since competency attainment involves a relationship with clients, the student has to exercise emotional creativity in the learning process. The demand for artistry poses a challenge. This chapter shows you how objectively identified competencies are attained in the ongoing and repetitive practice situation.

REVIEW OF THE SOCIAL WORK PRACTICE COMPETENCIES

The primary purpose of your social work education is the development of social work practice competencies that have been identified by the profession. As was discussed in Chapter 4, these competencies are grounded in professional knowledge and values and are comprised of various skills. There are nine social work competencies you will have to achieve, and the practice behaviors associated with these competencies are the skill sets you must develop.

To review, the nine competencies are (Council on Social Work Education [CSWE], 2015) as follows:

Competency 1—Demonstrate Ethical and Professional Behavior

Competency 2—Engage Diversity and Difference in Practice

Competency 3—Advance Human Rights and Social, Economic, and Environmental Justice

Competency 4—Engage in Practice-Informed Research and Research-Informed Practice

Competency 5—Engage in Policy Practice

Competency 6—Engage With Individuals, Families, Groups, Organizations, and Communities

Competency 7—Assess Individuals, Families, Groups, Organizations, and Communities

Competency 8—Intervene With Individuals, Families, Groups, Organizations, and Communities

Competency 9—Evaluate Practice With Individuals, Families, Groups, Organizations, and Communities

In meetings with clients, you are not thinking about what competency you are developing. You are actively listening, trying to focus on the client's feelings and issues in the moment and what the client needs from you. Some of your reflection about your current and future actions will occur in field instruction sessions. Further understanding will result from classroom experiences, including discussions, readings, and written assignments. Seizing opportunities to reflect on your skills will expand your repertoire of practice skills in the best interest of your clients.

This section offers you an opportunity to try something. Prepare a process recording of your interactions with a client: a group, individual, or family, using one of the outlines for process recording (see Appendix A for examples). Even if your program does not require process recordings, go ahead and try this. The process recording allows you to capture each moment with clients and to reflect on them.

Now that you have written it, read the process recording line by line, pausing along the way to identify your feelings, what the client was presenting, what was going on in the group or family, how you heard it, and what you missed. Look at each intervention you used and what you were trying to achieve. Assess its usefulness for the client. Practice behavior has to be applied correctly in order for it to be useful.

In the next section, several process recordings demonstrate how to reflect on your practice.

FIRST-YEAR COMPETENCY DEVELOPMENT EXEMPLARS

As you will recall, there are 29 suggested practice behaviors that accompany the nine competencies. To better understand how these behaviors are developed within your practice with clients, detailed case illustrations are presented.

CASE ILLUSTRATION 9.1

FAMILY ISSUES DISCUSSION GROUP FOR HOMELESS WOMEN WITH MENTAL ILLNESS

Marla is a first-year student in a comprehensive program that includes a shelter for homeless women—many of whom have mental illness. Their mental health struggles have contributed to their homelessness. Thirty-five women live at this site and take part in a group work day treatment program. Today, in this group of 8 members, Shauna talked about a visit home to her mother, from whom she had been estranged for three years. Her mother is also caring for Shauna's son, who is now 9.

Shauna told the group that as she got closer to the house she was thinking about turning around, but wanting to see where Mitchell was living kept her going. Although she had been seeing him under children's services supervision, it was never at home. "I know she is still angry at me for using and for being sick. She did not know I was sick. I did not know I was sick. I am afraid of what she tells him about me." Frances said that Shauna should be proud of herself for going ahead.

Shauna said that when she got there her mother was welcoming and hugged her. This surprised Shauna, who said it was hard for her to hug back because she still has anger at her mother for giving her "tough love" instead of bringing her to a hospital. Cecilia asked if her mom was getting help. Shauna said she assumed it is required by children's services.

Donna interjected that her sister still won't speak with her. Gloria asked why, and Donna noted that she couldn't keep a job and her sister resented her for it.

Marla stated, **"Family estrangement seems to be an issue for some members of the group."**

(Continued)

(Continued)

Shauna continued, saying that she was happy she had visited the house and that she was trying to fix the past and forgive her mother. Gloria asked about Mitchell. Shauna had to admit that he was being cared for better than what she could have done.

Marla asked, **"How does that make you feel about your mother?"** Shauna said, "Okay, grateful." Astria asked if Shauna resented her. She said, "Yes, that too."

Marla pointed out that it is important to recognize mixed feelings. Some members agreed. Karla said that she feels very happy that her sister is raising her daughter for her and loves her for it. She said she has no mixed feelings. Gloria said that she learned through her individual therapy that most people tend to have some mixed feelings, even toward those they love. Karla continued to say she does not feel this way. Donna asked Karla if the reverse were true—if she thought her sister would have mixed feelings toward her. "You said that your homelessness and illness made it hard for your family." Karla said that her sister loves her, and that's what it's about.

Marla asked if others wanted to report on seeing family recently.

Lily said she had been at a family wedding with her husband from whom she had been separated. She was so happy to see everybody and talked about how they might be getting back together. He had been abusive to her. She told the group he is in therapy and that he is working on his anger issues. She is cautiously optimistic. Karla noted, "If he loves you, maybe you can make it work." Donna said she does not think love is enough and pointed out that when love wants to control you, then it isn't love. Gloria said she believes each situation is different and asked Lily if she wants to go back or if he was pressuring her. Lily began to cry and said she is feeling a lot of pressure from his family and how much they like her, but she is not sure.

Marla said, **"You don't need to have answers now—even if others want answers."**

Others nodded in agreement. As the group's time was winding down, Marla said, **"There are many issues we can pick up on next time. You're all working so hard to help one another."**

Case Illustration 9.1 Preparation for Field Instruction

In preparation for field instruction, Marla reviewed her interventions to determine competency development and identify practice behavior. The following are Marla's reflections on her use of competencies:

"Family estrangement seems to be an issue for some members of the group."

Marla reflected on how she was universalizing a theme common to some in order to strengthen mutual aid. This intervention pertains to Competency 7: Assess Groups. She made an assessment that family estrangement is a common theme.

Additionally, Competency 8: Intervene With Groups pertains as well; she intervened to create connection.

The practice behavior she used related to assessment is as follows:

- Social workers collect, organize, and critically analyze and interpret information from clients and constituencies. (CSWE, 2015)

The practice behaviors she used related to intervention are as follows:

- Social workers implement interventions to achieve practice goals and enhance client and constituents' capacities.
- Social workers apply knowledge of human behavior and the social environment, person-in-environment, and other frameworks. (CSWE, 2015)

"How does that make you feel about your mother?"

Marla reflected on how she was hoping to focus on Shauna's ambivalent feelings. This intervention pertains to Competency 7: Assess Groups. Marla made an assessment that Shauna may have ambivalent feelings toward her mother.

Competency 8: Intervene With Groups also applies, as Marla asked an open-ended question that highlighted the client's feelings.

The practice behavior she used related to assessment is as follows:

- Social workers develop mutually agreed upon intervention goals based on the critical assessment of client strengths, needs, and challenges. (CSWE, 2015)

The practice behavior she used related to intervention is as follows:

- Social workers implement interventions to achieve practice goals and enhance clients and constituent capacities. (CSWE, 2015)

Marla pointed out that it is important to recognize mixed feelings.

In her reflections, Marla believed that people had to understand ambivalent feelings. She understood that for enhanced mental health, members needed to integrate the positive with the negative feelings they had about important people in their lives; otherwise, they would have relationship problems and exaggerated reactions. She was beginning to utilize diagnostic categories to guide her interventions.

This intervention pertains to Competency 7: Assess Individuals, as well as Competency 8: Intervene With Groups.

The practice behavior related to Marla's assessment is as follows:

- Social workers apply knowledge of human behavior and the social environment, person-in-environment, in the analysis of assessment data from clients. (CSWE, 2015)

The practice behaviors related to Marla's intervention are as follows:

- Social workers implement interventions to achieve practice goals and enhance capacities of clients. (CSWE, 2015)

Marla asked if others wanted to report on seeing family recently.

Marla knew it would be helpful to group members to tell their family stories, to strengthen the group, and to ensure that important material was not lost. This intervention pertains to Competency 8: Intervene With Groups.

The practice behavior she used related to intervention is as follows:

- Social workers implement interventions to achieve practice goals and enhance clients and constituent capacities. (CSWE, 2015)

"You don't need to have answers now—even if others want answers."

After Lily reported uncertainty about reconciling with her husband, Marla reflected on her response (shown here). The intervention pertained to Competency 8: Intervene With Groups. In this case, Marla reinforced group norms fostering members' autonomy and independent actions.

The practice behaviors she used related to intervention are as follows:

- Social workers negotiate, mediate, and advocate with clients.
- Social workers implement interventions to achieve practice goals and enhance client capacities. (CSWE, 2015)

"There are many issues we can pick up on next time. You're all working so hard to help one another."

This was the last intervention made to close the meeting. This intervention reflected Competency 8: Intervene With Groups.

The practice behavior related to Marla's intervention is as follows:

- Social workers facilitate transitions and endings that advance mutually agreed upon goals. (CSWE, 2015)

Practice behaviors are the generic way of viewing the specifics of practice in depth. In the foundation practice literature, Marla will find chapters on group work.

Discussion of group work (Glassman, 2008; Shulman, 2015) in the middle phase of practice will guide understanding of this group. They have passed through power and control issues, appear to be able to listen to one another, and are in the process of providing depth and support through relationship. For a student schooled in beginning group work, this excerpt will lead you in the direction of discovering what stage the group is in. Going further, consider group work norms, the role each member plays, and how each member connects to the group. For example, observe that in this meeting Gloria asks many open-ended questions. Perhaps Gloria provides glue for the group's cohesion.

The group work literature will focus on worker skills: being able to speak to the group as a whole, asking if others have something more to add to the conversation, and asking if their issues are being reflected are worker skills. You are trying to develop cohesion, communication, and understanding across a range of differences in personalities, diagnoses, and issues.

Marla's Field Instruction Meeting

Marla's field instructor, Roberto, told her that pointing to family estrangement as a common issue was a good way to work on creating the group's ability to understand one another. He asked if Marla thought that Shauna had shared everything about the visit home. Marla reflected that she may not have given her enough time. He suggested she ask next time if Shauna had more she wanted to add.

Roberto then asked Marla about Shauna's ambivalence. She said she knew Shauna had a diagnosis of borderline personality disorder and that she was trying to see if she could work on helping her connect the positive with the negative feelings. He commended Marla, saying it is not easy to do. She said she was not sure how hard to push. He told her she was right to let it go and speak about everyone having a different approach to life's issues.

Roberto asked Marla why she had pursued family situations and wanted to know how she was feeling during the discussion of parents and ambivalence. She said she was anxious because ambivalent feelings were hard for her to handle—especially with her brother. Roberto noted that she had moved away from Shauna's dilemma. What had she been feeling? "I felt its heaviness, returning to her mother's house, seeing her child there." Roberto asked, "Do you think there is some unfinished business in the group regarding Shauna's visit to her mother?" Marla said, "I guess so."

Marla asked when it is ineffective to stay with one person's issue too long. Roberto agreed that it is important to consider. "When you changed the subject to a group-oriented topic, you did it gracefully by transitioning from her family issue to a group family issue. Know that you are doing that and why. Understand that your own feelings were involved. That will direct you to go back to it next time. If not, you will never go back to it."

CASE ILLUSTRATION 9.2

LOBBY DAY PLANNING PROGRAM IN A COMMUNITY CENTER

Lauren is a senior-year spring semester student with a field placement in a community center. The state chapter of the National Association of Social Workers (NASW) is running Lobby Day and the center plans to participate. Lobby Day brings many constituent groups for a one-day event at their state capitol. Here they meet with legislators to advocate in support of programs that are important to them. One major program to support is universal pre-K. The other is expansion of housing options for seniors.

For Lauren's community organization project, her field instructor, Vicki, asked her to work with the Lobby Day committee cochairs to sign up participants. She told Lauren that seniors who wanted to sign up must have a doctor's clearance. Lauren thought it was harsh, but she has started to understand that some seniors do not want to accept their limitations. The program director discussed one senior who is too frail to take the trip but has a hard time accepting that her limitations put others and herself at risk. A long trip to the state capitol is a problem. There are several seniors with these issues, and Lauren must inform everyone who signs up that the event is subject to medical approval. This policy applies to everyone.

Lauren is looking forward to this event but feels badly for the seniors who cannot accept their limitations. However, she knows there are many stairs, they would have to walk long distances to get to the building, and bathrooms are not easily accessible. **Now Lauren sees the issues of the elderly, who have a hard time accepting where they are on the continuum and what this means for them.** They attend concerts, visit family, shop, and travel with help. Some of them require wheelchair service at airports.

One afternoon, Mr. Seijeck said he is signing up. He walks with a cane and has early Alzheimer's. His attendant tried to prod him away from the table, but he became angry at her. She motioned to Lauren to tell him he cannot go. **Lauren explained to Mr. Seijeck that he is free to sign up, but everyone who wants to attend is subject to obtaining a doctor's approval**. **She got nowhere with him, so she signed him up.** Her field instructor had told her not to get into a confrontation with any of the seniors. Take his name down and be done with it.

In supervision with Vicki, she and Lauren concluded that there might be some other way to involve the people who are unable to go. Vicki asked Lauren to put together a small group of seniors who can work on figuring out how to involve people who are unable to go.

Lauren reached out to several seniors, and Clara, Alexander, and William agreed to work with her on this task. At the subgroup meeting, she asked them what they thought about the fact that the center is limiting attendance. They agreed that not everyone should go. Clara said she is not able, although she would have been 10 years earlier. She accepts her limitations and is content and wouldn't try to get on a bus and worry the staff. Alexander said the group really needs a plan to involve everyone who is not going. One of the other interns, Pam, makes films. **Lauren presented the idea that the seniors can be part of a film that will be delivered to the state legislators.** They loved the idea. Lauren said that she would speak to the intern.

Vicki encouraged Lauren to proceed and said she would speak with Pam and Pam's field instructor to see if they could work it out.

Vicki reported back to Lauren after her meeting with Pam and her field instructor, and Pam was thrilled with the idea.

Lauren invited Pam to the next subgroup meeting. The members agreed to bring seniors to speak once Pam sets up the time frame. **Lauren offered to prep them for the camera,** and Pam said she would help everyone with that also. **Lauren asked the seniors to make a list of potential participants and then suggested they divide it amongst themselves and reach out to them.**

The seniors thought younger members of the community center should be included in the video to talk about Head Start and what it meant to them and their families, too. Lauren agreed and told them that **since she is working with the Head Start parents, she would bring this idea to the teens and staff.**

Case Illustration 9.2 Preparation for Field Instruction

To prepare for field instruction, Lauren reviewed her actions and reflected on her use of competencies and practice behaviors.

Now Lauren sees the issues of the elderly, who have a hard time accepting where they are on the continuum and what this means for them.

This reflects Competency 7: Assess Individuals. Lauren has incorporated theories of aging, including reflections about acceptance of the aging process.

This intervention also reflects Competency 6: Engage With Individuals. In consciously including each group member, Lauren is fostering the development of mutual aid.

The practice behavior reflecting assessment is as follows:

- Social workers apply knowledge of human behavior and the social environment, person-in-environment, in the analysis of data from clients and constituencies. (CSWE, 2015)

The practice behavior reflecting engagement is as follows:

- Social workers use empathy, reflection, and interpersonal skills to effectively engage diverse clients and constituencies. (CSWE, 2015)

Lauren explained to Mr. Seijeck that he is free to sign up, but everyone who wants to attend is subject to obtaining a doctor's approval. She got nowhere with him, so she signed him up.

This represents Competency 8: Intervene With Individuals. She chooses not to argue with him about his potential participation in the event in order not to embarrass him and to preserve his membership and feeling of belonging in the group and community center.

The practice behavior reflecting engagement is as follows:

- Social workers use empathy, reflection, and interpersonal skills to effectively engage diverse clients and constituencies. (CSWE, 2015)

Lauren presented the idea that the seniors can be part of a film that will be delivered to the state legislators.

This reflection represents Competency 8: Intervene With Organizations. Making a film and including various agency participants in it strengthens the organizational goals of the agency.

The practice behaviors reflecting intervention with organizations are as follows:

- Social workers negotiate, mediate, and advocate with and on behalf of clients and constituencies.
- Social workers implement interventions to achieve practice goals and enhance client and constituent capacities. (CSWE, 2015)

Lauren invited Pam to the next subgroup meeting.

Further reflection upon this next intervention shows Competency 8: Intervene With Organizations. By creating interaction among constituent groups, Lauren is strengthening the agency's organizational goals while enhancing individual growth.

The practice behavior reflecting intervention is as follows:

- Social workers implement interventions to achieve practice goals and enhance client and constituent capacities. (CSWE, 2015)

Lauren offered to prep them for the camera.

This intervention shows Competency 8: Intervene With Groups. This action assists them in heightening their self-presentations before a camera.

The practice behavior reflecting intervention is as follows:

- Social workers implement interventions to achieve practice goals and enhance client and constituent capacities. (CSWE, 2015)

Lauren asked the seniors to make a list of potential participants and then suggested they divide it amongst themselves and reach out to them.

This reflects Competency 8: Intervene With Groups. These additional tasks enhance members' involvement in and ownership of the project.

The practice behavior reflecting intervention is as follows:

- Social workers implement interventions to achieve practice goals and enhance client and constituent capacities. (CSWE, 2015)

Since she is working with the Head Start parents, she would bring this idea to the teens and staff.

This reflects Competency 8: Intervene With Groups. Lauren models for the group how to involve others in activities that may foster their well-being.

The practice behavior showing intervention is as follows:

- Social workers negotiate, mediate, and advocate with and on behalf of clients and constituencies. (CSWE, 2015)

Lauren's Field Instruction Meeting

Vicki affirmed the making of a film to deliver to state legislators was clearly a way for members to have their voices heard. Then she asked Lauren to talk about what she has been learning in this new role. Lauren said that she found it very interesting to consider interventions in terms of the competency framework. Lauren told Vicki she was working on organizing goals. Vicki said, "But you are also working on personal issues. Look at how Clara says she accepts her limitations." Lauren said that although she registered this, she did not know what to say about it. Vicki asked her if there was something more she could have said. "I could have affirmed her and asked if the others felt that way. But I thought it might impede the organizational work we were doing." Vicki told her that she did not necessarily have to say anything—just nod her head in agreement—and reminded her that this was something to be used later.

Vicki stated this looked like a simple meeting, but it wasn't. Lauren agreed that there was so much going on, and she mentioned how glad she is to have thought of Pam and the film idea. Vicki asked how she was feeling. She said, "Desperate to please and anxious about dealing with those who are unable to go. It is not something I encounter with people I know. You go where you want. Limitations are not physical. They are about money, time, and schedule. It gives me another perspective." Vicki asked if Lauren had thought about policy implications. She had not. Vicki stated that policy affects lives daily—for example, policy determines where a child will go if there is no Head Start program.

Vicki asked how Lauren felt about Mr. Seijeck approaching her and being unrelenting. Lauren admitted to being put off by him yet feeling supported by his caretaker who tried to steer him away and then Vicki's words: "Don't have a confrontation with anyone." Vicki pointed out that managing a difficult client—even when he is not your client—is something that must be done in a system and is a much-needed skill. Vicki pointed out that Clara's frame of mind about her own limitations will come in handy later on.

Vicki commended Lauren for her tenacity and for following through with the seniors to work on the film and asked how Mr. Seijeck can be included. She suggested Lauren speak with the caregiver to see if he can be prepped to say a few words.

Vicki noted that the competencies Lauren identified are practice-based, except for one focused on assessment. She asked if there is a policy competency contained in her work as well. Lauren agreed that as she gets more involved in the lobby program she becomes more cognizant of how much she has to know about government programs and their impact on people in the community.

In the preceding process recordings and their review, the complexities of social work practice are evident. Take note of the progression in the students' learning. With each new intervention, the students and field instructors weave in a concept. This process paves the way for further new interventions and newer complex weaves.

MOVING FORWARD WITH FOUNDATION COMPETENCIES

The nine competencies attained by foundation first-year and senior-year bachelor in social work (BSW) students, which are demonstrated in their performance of the suggested 29 practice behaviors, provide the foundation for future direction. A senior-year student with a BSW degree is capable of obtaining employment to provide social service in agency settings performing generic social work under supervision. A master in social work (MSW) student who has completed a foundation first year is capable of moving into a second-year area of specialization in which competency development is deepened by performing specialization-based practice behaviors. At the end of the foundation level, students have developed the full range of foundation practice skills, including the ability to utilize empathy, knowledge, and values to engage clients; to develop and present professional assessments; and to apply all relevant aspects of knowledge and social work values to intervene with and on behalf of clients to meet purposeful goals. First and foremost, students should be able to respond professionally to the situation at hand and utilize professional supervision to direct their interventions.

The development of these competencies at the foundation level creates the opportunity for BSW and first-year students to enter the advanced year of the MSW program. Some BSW graduates may delay securing the MSW degree in order to obtain more experience. Yet for all involved, the foundation year lays the groundwork for progression into future MSW education.

SOCIAL WORK CODE OF ETHICS AS FOUNDATION FOR COMPETENT PRACTICE

In addition to developing social work competencies, students must adhere to ethical standards when dealing with clients and others. A range of ethical issues is presented in the first-year process recordings illustrated in this chapter. Several highlights of ethical issues the students are dealing with in their process recordings are shown in the following case illustrations.

CASE ILLUSTRATION 9.3

FAMILY ISSUES GROUP FOR HOMELESS WOMEN WITH MENTAL ILLNESS—SOCIAL WORK ETHICS

The group members in Marla's process recording—homeless women with mental illness—represent a stigmatized population. Shauna talked about the stigma and how her mother did not acknowledge she needed psychiatric help, giving her tough love instead.

Marla tried to strengthen mutual aid. This is a value regarding social conscience and the fact that members care for one another. This supports the value base that emphasizes the importance of human relationships (NASW, 2008). In this group meeting, supported relationships are those with family and among group members.

Throughout the group meeting, clients' self-determination and improved self-esteem are underlying themes that reflect the student's ability to work within social

(Continued)

(Continued)

work values that include harnessing clients' strengths. The ethical principle is as follows:

1.02 Self-Determination (NASW, 2008)

Social workers respect and promote the right of clients to self determination and assist clients in their efforts to identify and clarify their goals. Social workers may limit clients' right to self determination when, in the social workers' professional judgment, clients' actions or potential actions pose a serious, foreseeable, and imminent risk to themselves or others. (p. 4)

CASE ILLUSTRATION 9.4

LOBBY DAY PROGRAM PLANNING IN A COMMUNITY CENTER—SOCIAL WORK ETHICS

In working within the community center to facilitate participation in Lobby Day, Lauren must work creatively to enhance client self-determination. This is more important in light of the fact that the agency will not allow frail senior citizens to make the trip because they will be unable to handle the necessary navigation around the state capitol buildings. The ethical principle here is as follows:

1.02 Self Determination (NASW, 2008)

Social workers respect and promote the right of clients to self determination and assist clients in their efforts to identify and clarify their goals. Social workers may limit clients' right to self determination when, in the social workers' professional judgment, clients' actions or potential actions pose a serious, foreseeable, and imminent risk to themselves or others. (p. 4)

Lauren, with help from her field instructor, entertained an alternative way for seniors to have their views heard in the state by asking another intern to develop a film, including community center participants who cannot attend. This strategy, growing out of adherence to the principle of client self-determination, enables involvement of Head Start parents as well—many of whom are unable to take a day off from caring for their children to ride to the state capitol. Together with the seniors, they are committed to pre-K education and affordable housing, which they want to convey emphatically to state leaders.

Lauren further facilitated their self-determination by involving the seniors group in outreach to other participants and in offering to help them prepare for the camera. These tasks, along with further discussion, create ways of including teens in the process and broaden the intergenerational component as per the wishes of the senior citizens.

By being involved in the planning of a lobby program, Lauren is promoting social justice as required by the NASW *Code of Ethics* (NASW, 2008, p. 4). This role is detailed further as follows:

6.04 Social and Political Action (NASW, 2008)

(a) Social workers should engage in social and political action that seeks to ensure that all people have equal access to the resources, employment, services, and opportunities they require to meet their basic human needs and to develop fully. (p. 15)

The process Lauren uses to involve constituents reflects adherence to the importance of human relationships (NASW, 2008, p. 5).

SUMMARY

This chapter has shown you how to reflect on your practice with client systems and scrutinize your progress toward competency attainment. Each intervention drawn from students' process recordings was analyzed in regard to its competency and related practice behavior(s), which serve as models for your own reflections and analyses. Remember to use the nine competencies from the *Educational Policy and Accreditation Standards* (CSWE, 2015) to guide your reflections. How a field instructor and student review competency development was demonstrated as well, which can prepare you for your own meetings with your field instructor. The chapter concluded with further reflection on the NASW *Code of Ethics* (NASW, 2008) and its applicability in each of the process recordings that were reviewed.

Chapter 10 uses a similar review to show how students in second-year MSW field placements deepen competency attainment within the framework of their area of specialization.

Chapter 10

Advanced Competencies in the Second Year

INTRODUCTION

The challenge for students in second-year master in social work (MSW) specializations is to build on foundation competencies while applying the practice behaviors of their chosen specializations. The purpose is to develop depth in achieving competencies by using the practice behaviors of the specialization. In a similar manner to the foundation year, students must demonstrate advanced competency in the minute to minute affective exchange with clients. However, in having achieved foundation competency, the second-year student will begin the task again with greater confidence in engaging clients and sustaining relationships. This chapter shows how advanced second-year competencies are reached in the ongoing and repetitive practice situation.

GETTING STARTED

There are two helpful things to do as you get started in your second year: Identify your school's specialization curriculum, and gain a full understanding of your chosen specialization area.

Start With Your School's Specialization Curriculum

In the second year, students are expected to build a deeper skill set pertaining to their specialization. Thus, while competencies for second year are the same as those for first year, the practice behaviors identified differ and are related to a specific specialization. These practice behaviors are determined by your school's curriculum and areas of specialization.

Each school develops the specializations students may select and provides a skill set framework of practice behaviors that is used to measure attainment of the competency at this advanced level. Schools' specializations will be organized in various ways—by problem area, population, or method. Some schools may have only one specialization. Some problem areas might be substance abuse treatment, poverty and homelessness, domestic abuse, child welfare, or advanced generalist. A population framework may include social work practice with people with disabilities, children and families, rural populations, or people with mental illness. A methods framework is built upon social work's tradition of social casework, social group work, community organization, administration, policy, and research.

There may also be certificate programs in your school that will frame your specialization experiences, such as social work practice in gerontology, clinical practice with the military, and child welfare practice with families of color.

Understand Your Specialization Area

Your choice of specialization will be based upon your strengths, where you wish to serve, and what you feel driven to learn. It is important to understand the requirements within the specialization. This includes knowing the coursework you must take and the range of field work experiences that is available. Although field work assignments will support a specialization, the relationship between a student's field assignments and specialization never fully align. The extent to which you integrate knowledge with practice depends in part on how you use your course materials, written papers, and assigned tasks at the agency. Your proactivity is needed to determine how practice and research courses inform your field experience and deepen your competency attainment in the specialization.

Studying your school's field manual, with a focus on second-year learning experiences, ensures that you are on track. Reviewing your school's midyear and final evaluation guidelines and format also helps to define the track you are on.

SECOND-YEAR SPECIALIZATION EXEMPLARS

The following case illustrations should focus your preparation for second year and help you reflect on what you are doing and learning throughout your second-year field placement. Several typical situations seen in field placement experiences will be illustrated, which all apply beyond the particular specialization. Competencies will be reviewed and practice behaviors associated with each competency will be identified.

CASE ILLUSTRATION 10.1

SOCIAL WORK TREATMENT FOR ALCOHOL AND SUBSTANCE ABUSE SPECIALIZATION

Lucas was placed at an urban alcohol and substance abuse treatment program where he runs several groups and has individual clients. This group meeting of nine men were talking about the challenges they experience in trying to stay away from people associated with their past drug use.

Julian talked about his ex-girlfriend and how he has to deal with her in order to see his children. However, he fears she is using again and doesn't know what to do about it because he does not want to drag the children through more difficulties. Yet he doesn't want them around this environment. Derek urged him to gain custody of his kids. Mauricio noted that the best thing that happened for him was when his mother-in-law took the children from him and his wife, which forced them to get help. Eddie agreed.

Lucas asked Julian how he has been doing given this difficult time. Julian said that he is afraid of being laid off from his construction job because the constant rainfalls have prevented them from working on a site. Sam said he is facing similar problems. The restoration of his neighborhood may lead to rent hikes on the restaurant, which creates a lot of uncertainty.

Lucas pointed out, "On top of having to deal with your own personal issues related to sobriety, external ones are additional factors."

Eddie said that his father with whom he lives was planning to retire from his law firm and move to Arizona. However, Eddie knows that his father isn't going yet because he does not want to leave Eddie alone—he worries about him. His father, an alcoholic, has been sober for 30 years.

Julian asked if there is any extra reason for his father to be concerned. Mauricio urged Eddie to tell the group about the latest incident. Eddie said he had a small group over to his house to watch a hockey game. The guys brought some beer, which was okay with Eddie. A couple of their girlfriends came too. He made sliders for everyone and brought in other catered food. It was healthy; it was great. His father was out and when he came back and saw the beer, he freaked out. Eddie said he had not prepared him for it. Derek asked him how he handled the drinking. Eddie said that his approach had been to find recipes and make the food, something he never could have done in the past. He said that at

(Continued)

(Continued)

Alcoholics Anonymous (AA) people talk about parties, too. Mauricio pointed out that Eddie's father does not allow booze in his house, and that was also why he freaked out.

Lucas asked if Eddie had been pushing his father's button on purpose. Derek noted that he does that too, saying, "People are watching out for you, but it's the same people who watched helplessly while you were screwing up your life, and we did not listen." Mauricio pointed out that Eddie's father has never allowed liquor in the house since he became sober.

A discussion ensued about the complex relationships they have with family. Sam talked about repairing the relationship with his mother and how at times he tries to avoid taking in what she says—like the old days.

The group meeting continued with members talking about testing their close relationships and some of the guilt and shame they feel about what they put others through.

Later on in the meeting, as the group is drawing to a close for the day, Lucas **pointed out that these are bound to be recurring issues and thanked the members for bringing up these issues and for their honesty and openness.**

Case Illustration 10.1 Preparation for Field Instruction

To prepare for field instruction, Lucas reviewed his interventions to determine competency development and identify practice behaviors.

Lucas asked Julian how he has been doing given this difficult time.

This statement reflects Competency 8: Intervene With Groups. Lucas underscores the emotional stress being placed on Julian and echoes the group's show of support for Julian.

This statement also reflects Competency 7: Assess Individuals. Lucas uses knowledge of substance abuse and treatment implications to reflect on the group member's difficulties.

The practice behavior associated with intervention with groups within the substance abuse treatment concentration is as follows:

- Social workers help clients resolve problems utilizing group supports to assist members in recognizing triggers that may undermine sobriety. (Council on Social Work Education [CSWE], 2015)

The practice behaviors reflecting assessment within the substance abuse treatment concentration are as follows:

- Social workers utilize conceptual frameworks about recidivism and unresolved historical relationships to guide the processes of assessment, intervention, and evaluation.
- Social workers critique and apply knowledge of medical factors related to addictions to understand person and environment. (CSWE, 2015)

Lucas pointed out, "On top of having to deal with your own personal issues related to sobriety, external ones are additional factors."

Lucas determines he is showing Competency 7: Assess within the substance abuse treatment concentration. He has assessed that the group members function in the context of the environment and that they will work out ways to support each other in dealing with environmental factors. He also determines he is showing Competency 8: Intervene With Groups in substance abuse treatment. Lucas focuses the members' attention on the difference between stressors related to sobriety, and stressors that are interpersonal in order to enhance their mutual aid supports.

The practice behaviors reflecting assessment within the substance abuse treatment concentration are as follows:

- Social workers collect, organize, and interpret client data pertaining to group formation, and family factors that help or hinder sobriety.
- Social workers assess client strengths and limitations with regard to biopsychosocial factors influencing sobriety. (CSWE, 2015)

The practice behavior reflecting intervention within the substance abuse treatment concentration is as follows:

- Social workers implement prevention interventions that enhance client capacities for insight and the enhancement of vocational and educational factors to enhance self-esteem. (CSWE, 2015)

The next comment is to Eddie. Lucas asked if Eddie had been pushing his father's button on purpose.

This reflects Competency 7: Assess in the substance abuse treatment concentration. Lucas believes that Eddie falls back on confrontational and provocative behavior. He also knows that this is a group phenomenon and sees it as part of stage theory of group development—a common issue for all the members. He asks the question to raise everyone's awareness.

This statement also demonstrates Competency 8: Intervene With the Group. Lucas utilizes his knowledge of group development and group norms and intervenes to guide the group.

The practice behaviors reflecting assessment are as follows:

- Social workers utilize conceptual frameworks to guide the processes of assessment, intervention, and evaluation which pertain to conflictual and self-destructive relationships.
- Social workers critique and apply knowledge to understand person and environment.
- Social workers assess client strengths and limitations to include biopsychosocial factors that support or hinder sobriety and recovery. (CSWE, 2015)

The practice behavior reflecting intervention is as follows:

- Social workers implement prevention interventions that enhance client capacities which include self-betterment, enhanced self-esteem, and recognition of self-destructive patterns. (CSWE, 2015)

To wrap up the session, Lucas pointed out that these are bound to be recurring issues and thanked the members for bringing up these issues and for their honesty and openness.

Lucas is showing Competency 7: Assess the Group. He knows that sobriety is attained through repetitive efforts and that family issues will recur. He is showing Competency 8: Intervene With Individuals. He wants to emphasize the realities about the hard work they are undertaking and encourage their continued trust in one another.

The practice behavior demonstrating assessment is as follows:

- Social workers assess client strengths and limitations recognizing the difficulties in changing dysfunctional patterns that impeded growth. (CSWE, 2015)

The practice behavior reflecting intervention is as follows:

- Social workers implement prevention interventions that enhance client capacities. (CSWE, 2015)

Lucas's Field Instruction Meeting

Linda is Lucas's field instructor. A major effort at this program has been to develop a training program for group work in substance abuse treatment at which

Lucas participated. Linda credited Lucas for understanding Julian's difficulties in trying to keep a job and universalizing this issue to the group in order to maximize support.

She then asked Lucas to share his reaction about Julian's report that his ex-girlfriend was possibly using drugs again. Lucas said he was concerned, but since Julian did not see it as an immediate problem, he let it go. Linda advised Lucas to talk further with Julian about the suspected drug use because they must decide if there is reason to file a report with children's services. She suggested Lucas contact Julian, and if he is unable to make an assessment, the three of them should meet almost immediately.

Lucas left the meeting with Linda and called Julian, saying he would like him to come by later in the afternoon. Julian agreed and noted, "You got worried about my ex, right?"

Lucas returned to tell Linda he felt Julian was relieved that he called. Linda noted that Julian put the issue out in the group to see if a follow-up was warranted. They planned Lucas's meeting with Julian, and Linda agreed to be in the office to meet with Julian herself.

They continued to talk about the group meeting.

Linda asked Lucas to talk about the incident the group raised with Eddie having a party that frightened his father. Lucas said he sees that Eddie is unaware of how provocative he can be. This was confirmed when Julian pushed Eddie to talk about the party incident in the group. Lucas said he felt that the members' supportive abilities as well as their understanding of one another's dysfunctional behaviors showed him their intelligence and motivation. Lucas said he took a chance asking Eddie if he was pushing his father's buttons because "I believed the group understood that and I wanted to help them raise the issue." Linda agreed and stated, "Your recognition of the group's latent process is on target, and you used it well." She agreed that the members are able to talk about the way family would be suspicious and the necessity for repairing relationships that have been damaged by their lack of credibility.

Later in their meeting, Linda pointed to Lucas's comment about issues recurring and repeating and that the support he gave to the members was important to let them know not to be frustrated by recurring themes or backslides.

Linda asked Lucas to consider the level of the group's cohesion and what some of the difficult future topics may be. Lucas believes they are cohesive. Yet he has many feelings and opinions about how each member should be dealing with historical negative relationships. This is especially true for the men with children who have lost custody to their partner due to addiction. He noted that some of the men are ambivalent. On one hand, they would like their children back and do not trust their ex. On the other hand, they also feel that gaining custody would burden their aging mothers. In addition, most of the members lack confidence in their own parenting abilities, having had difficult or nonexistent relationships with fathers. Linda asked how this question may be raised. Lucas noted that members have hinted about their parenting concerns, but nothing more has been said up until now. Further discussion ensued about how conflict in the father role has been a typical issue with male addicts and the potential for using group supports to strengthen members' desires to be effective fathers.

CASE ILLUSTRATION 10.2

CLINICAL SOCIAL WORK SPECIALIZATION

Kendra has a field placement in a partial hospital program for persons with mental illness. Her client Tonya is a 28-year-old who was diagnosed with schizophrenia after a break in her senior year at college. She was heading to medical school in a research-based combined MD–PhD program. Her father, with whom she had a good relationship, was a doctor and recently died from complications of heart disease. Her relationship with her mother is complex. The loss of her father poses a major threat to her well-being.

At this session, Tonya talked about her cousin Jack and her sister Wanda who helped her get through the funeral and wake. Her brother Bill is 10 years older, and she feels he and his wife rejected her at the time of her break. Tonya expressed pain and disappointment about that. They spend no time with her, and she longs for a chance to see their young children. She described seeing them at the funeral.

Kendra had wondered if she should go to the funeral with Tonya. However, after discussion with her field instructor they agreed it was unnecessary since she had family and two friends from the day program also attending. Kendra continues to feel bad about not going.

Kendra asked Tonya what happened when she saw her brother Bill. "He tried to talk to me, but he looked worried and did not know what to say. It is as if I can give him and his kids a disease. His wife is super mean. My sister agrees with me and told my brother that she is nasty. My father used to say not to hold a grudge but to do the best for myself."

Tonya talked about trying to return to college and dropping a lab course because it was too hard for her to focus. Kendra **wondered what would happen if she were to try to go back to school now. "Have you ever brought this up with your doctor?"** Tonya said no, but she will think about it.

Kendra continued, **"Tell me about your father's funeral."** Tonya described how the minister talked about him as a doctor but not so much about him as a father. "No one really understands how good he was to me. I think he felt guilty." Kendra asked, "Why guilty?" I think because my mother was afraid to have me live at the house, even though I take my meds."

Kendra said, **"You must be so sad now."** She admitted that she is. Kendra asked, **"Have you gotten out of bed?"** Tonya replied she has not except for the session. **"Have you eaten?"** "I did." **"Like what?"** Tonya said she had chips in her room and that Donna came to get her but she yelled at her.

Her reaction scared Kendra, and she asked, "Why yell?" "Because I am mad, and I don't have my father to talk to." At that moment, Kendra understood that anyone in her situation would be angry and sad. She tried to normalize it by saying, **"Tonya, it's common to be mad when someone close to you dies."** Kendra wasn't sure if Tonya heard her or not.

Tonya then jumped to the topic of a trust fund. "He said he was going to leave me a trust fund, but then it would make me lose my benefits. He left it to my sister to take care of me." **Kendra asked how she feels,** and Tonya said she is okay with it since she trusts her sister. Kendra did not pursue this.

For now, Kendra wanted to be sure she was eating and had people to be with. **She suggested Tonya find Donna and go to the cafeteria with her.** But Tonya did not want to go to the cafeteria. Since they are both in her poetry group, Kendra said, **"How about I ask Donna to bring some food up for you? You know she wants to help you, Tonya."** Tonya agreed. Kendra said she would talk to her tomorrow.

Kendra wondered if Tonya will be taken advantage of by her family. She wondered how to protect Tonya's interests, since she is so vulnerable.

Kendra's other concern is that Tonya not deteriorate from this. Should Kendra contact the psychiatrist to check her meds or increase her meds? Tonya would hate the idea of increasing her meds, but in this case it might be warranted.

Case Illustration 10.2 Preparation for Field Instruction

Before field instruction, Kendra sat down and reviewed her interventions with Tonya to evaluate her own competency development and to identify relevant practice behaviors.

Kendra asked Tonya what happened when she saw her brother Bill.

Kendra concludes that she is demonstrating Competency 6: Engage With Individuals. She would like Tonya to tell her story of a crisis event. She feels she is also demonstrating Competency 8: Intervene With Individuals. Kendra recognizes that it is necessary for Tonya to discuss her painful issues in order to preserve her mental health during this crisis time.

The practice behavior demonstrating engagement is as follows:

- "Attend to the interpersonal and contextual factors affecting the therapeutic alliance." (Simmons College School of Social Work, 2015, p. 4)

The practice behavior demonstrating intervention is as follows:

- "Critically evaluate, select, and apply best practices and evidence-based interventions." (Simmons College School of Social Work, 2015, p. 4)

Kendra wondered what would happen if she were to try to go back to school now. "Have you ever brought this up with your doctor?"

This was a response to Tonya's statement about returning to college. Kendra does not know if the client's illness will impede her ability to maintain focus in school. Her exploratory questions lay the foundation for involving the client's therapeutic team. Kendra notes she is demonstrating Competency 8: Intervene With Individuals. She is letting the client know that her doctor should be consulted. Competency 7: Assess Individuals is being demonstrated because she needs input from the client's doctor.

The practice behavior demonstrating intervention is as follows:

- "Critically evaluate, select, and apply best practices and evidence-based interventions." (Simmons College School of Social Work, 2015, p. 4)

The practice behavior demonstrating assessment is as follows:

- "Select and modify appropriate intervention strategies based on continuous clinical assessment." (Simmons College School of Social Work, 2015, p. 4)

Kendra continued, "Tell me about your father's funeral."

She knows the importance of hearing the client's story about the funeral and the family and reflects that she is demonstrating Competency 8: Intervene With Individuals. She also realizes the therapeutic value to the client of sharing feelings about her loss, which demonstrates Competency 7: Assess.

The practice behavior demonstrating intervention is as follows:

- "Critically evaluate, select, and apply best practices and evidence-based interventions." (Simmons College School of Social Work, 2015, p. 4)

The practice behavior demonstrating assessment is as follows:

- "Select and modify appropriate intervention strategies based on continuous clinical assessment." (Simmons College School of Social Work, 2015, p. 4)

Kendra said, "You must be so sad now." She admitted that she is. Kendra asked, "Have you gotten out of bed?" Tonya replied she has not except for the session. "Have you eaten?" "I did." "Like what?"

In her concern for the Tonya's well-being, Kendra realizes the interplay between mental status and nutrition. This demonstrates Competency 7: Assess Individuals. Kendra knows that loss of appetite is one symptom of depression. She is demonstrating Competency 8: Intervene With Individuals. By bringing up the necessity for Tonya to eat, Kendra is supporting the client's ability to take care of herself.

The practice behavior demonstrating assessment is as follows:

- "Select and modify appropriate intervention strategies based on continuous clinical assessment." (Simmons College School of Social Work, 2015, p. 4)

The practice behavior demonstrating intervention is as follows:

- "Critically evaluate, select, and apply best practices and evidence-based interventions." (Simmons College School of Social Work, 2015, p. 4)

"Tonya, it's common to be mad when someone close to you dies."

Kendra's effort is to normalize the client's anger and sadness, which demonstrates Competency 8: Intervene With Individuals and Competency 7: Assess Individuals.

The practice behaviors reflecting **assessment** are as follows:

- "Synthesize and differentially apply theories of human behavior and the social environment to guide clinical practice." (Simmons College School of Social Work, 2015, p. 4)
- "Use bio-psycho-social-spiritual theories and multi-axial diagnostic classification systems in the formulation of comprehensive assessments." (Simmons College School of Social Work, 2015, p. 3)

The practice behavior demonstrating intervention is as follows:

- "Critically evaluate, select, and apply best practices and evidence-based interventions." (Simmons College School of Social Work, 2015, p. 4)

Kendra asked how she feels.

Tonya's father left a trust fund to her sister for Tonya's care. Kendra is aware that a vulnerable client may be taken advantage of. This comment shows Competency 3: Advance Human Rights and Social, Economic, and Environmental Justice.

The practice behavior of advance human rights and justice is as follows:

- "Use knowledge of the effects of oppression, discrimination, and historical trauma on client and client systems to guide treatment planning, intervention and advocacy." (Simmons College School of Social Work, 2015, p. 2)

She suggested Tonya find Donna and go to the cafeteria with her. But Tonya did not want to go to the cafeteria. Kendra said, "How about I ask Donna to bring some food up for you? You know she wants to help you, Tonya."

Kendra believes the client needs structure and supports to get through this difficult loss. Her comments show Competency 7: Assess Individuals and Competency 1: Demonstrate Ethical and Professional Behavior.

The practice behavior of assessment is as follows:

- "Apply differential and multiaxial diagnoses" (Simmons College School of Social Work, 2015, p. 4)

The practice behavior of demonstrate ethical and professional behavior is as follows:

- "Develop, manage and maintain therapeutic relationships with clients within the person in environment and strengths perspectives." (Simmons College School of Social Work, 2015, p. 4)

Kendra wondered if Tonya will be taken advantage of by her family.

Kendra realizes her client's vulnerabilities. Her concern shows Competency 3: Advance Human Rights and Social, Economic, and Environmental Justice.

The practice behavior of advance human rights and justice is as follows:

- "Use knowledge of the effects of oppression, discrimination and historical trauma on client and client systems to guide treatment planning, intervention, and advocacy." (Simmons College School of Social Work, 2015, p. 2)

Kendra's other concern is that Tonya not deteriorate from this loss.

Having assessed the crisis of her client with schizophrenia, Kendra is appropriately concerned and questions how to use the team to support the client. This shows Competency 7: Assess Individuals and Competency 8: Intervene With Individuals.

The practice behavior of assessment and intervention is as follows:

- "Select and modify appropriate intervention strategies based on continuous clinical assessment." (Simmons College School of Social Work, 2015, p. 4)

Kendra's Field Instruction Meeting

Kendra brought her process recording to Fern, her field instructor. Fern started the meeting by affirming that she had done a good job trying to get Tonya to eat and in normalizing the grief and sadness she was feeling.

Fern noted, "You conclude that her reactions are typical grief. Was there any indication there might be more than that? I am asking because in the end you wonder about increasing her meds. Did you observe any further symptoms?" Kendra said she thought the discussion of the trust fund was somewhat random. Fern interpreted, "Meaning she should not be talking about issues of money?" Kendra agreed. Fern asked, "Why do you think she would talk about money?" "She lost her father—he took care of her." "Yes, and a trust fund?" Kendra reflected that it will take care of Tonya. Right.

Then Fern asked, "Can you tell me a little bit about when you had to deal with the death of a close family member or friend?" Kendra noted that her uncle had died last year. "What were the circumstances?" He succumbed to MS at age 50. Prior to that, he had been quite vibrant. Fern asked her what the immediate family discussed when he died. She went on to recount issues with the disease. Fern asked about wife and children. He had a child in college and was divorced. Fern asked if her parents talked about this. "Yes, they had concerns about the kind of insurance he had left for the children, and they could not find out." After Fern acknowledged that this must have been hard for Kendra, she wondered if any of this was familiar to her. Kendra then agreed that Tonya broaching the subject was something common that people do when someone dies. Fern said, "Yes, but she has no one to talk to about it, and that must be more difficult for her, so she had to bring it up to you. The red flag was raised for you that she could be taken advantage of. Your own historical experience in this case helped you to have this concern."

Fern noted in the process recording that the client registered lack of connection to her brother and asked Kendra, "How do you see this in family dynamic terms?" Kendra noted he is much older and likely grew up removed from Tonya. They seem disengaged and distant from each other. "Yes and with the father gone, the brother is not apt to start now." Fern noted Tonya feels close to her sister and in due time that relationship will be clearer.

She also pointed out that Tonya did not talk about her mother and told Kendra that it is important to learn more about that relationship. "Did Tonya go to the house after the funeral?" Kendra agreed to follow up on this.

Fern asked Kendra how she was feeling. "I feel very sad for her. I still feel badly that I did not attend the funeral." Fern asked, "Whose need is this?" Kendra admitted Tonya did not need her there. Fern said, "It is okay to understand your need and try to reflect on where it is coming from." Kendra said she is not afraid to go to funerals and that in her culture even kids go. Fern said that this is not the case in her culture. An interesting discussion ensued between the two about death and culture and how to help Tonya.

They agreed Kendra will speak to the psychiatrist and have Tonya meet with her as a preventive measure.

SOCIAL WORK CODE OF ETHICS AS FOUNDATION FOR COMPETENT PRACTICE

In addition to advancing your competencies, you must continue to practice ethically. A range of ethical issues is presented in the second-year process recordings illustrated in this chapter. Several highlights of ethical issues the students are dealing with in their process recordings are presented in the following case illustrations.

CASE ILLUSTRATION 10.3

SOCIAL WORK TREATMENT FOR ALCOHOL AND SUBSTANCE ABUSE SPECIALIZATION

Recall from Lucas's case illustration that Julian shared his fear that his ex-girlfriend is using drugs again and was concerned about his children who are in her custody. In Lucas's field instruction meeting, several potential ethical issues Lucas will have to deal with directly were discussed, which are presented here.

The first ethical issue is immediate and has to do with the welfare of Julian's children should his ex-girlfriend be using drugs again. Lucas must consider whether or not there is a need to file a report with children's services and if filing such a report is an immediate requirement. It became necessary for Lucas and his field instructor to plan an immediate discussion with Julian about the suspected drug use and the steps to be taken in protecting the children. The ethical principle is concerned with the constraints of self-determination and the interests of protecting clients.

1.02 Self-Determination (National Association of Social Workers [NASW], 2008)

Social workers may limit clients' right to self determination when, in the social workers' professional judgment, clients' actions or potential actions pose a serious, foreseeable, and imminent risk to themselves or others. (p. 4)

In this case, because of his prior history, Julian may not be able to file a report with children's services. As mandated reporters, social work students must become familiar with laws that protect children and procedures to follow as mandated reporters. In addition to recognizing ethical issues, this situation requires the student to reflect upon the differences between ethical practice and practicing within the law.

Lucas should also be learning that within the social work practice in the alcohol and substance abuse treatment specialization, issues related to child welfare are common, and there will be many clients whose children are or have been in care. Students will have to learn about the various ethical decisions that have to be made with and sometimes for many of their clients.

The second ethical issue centers on economic matters related to unemployment. Julian may need advocacy in filing for unemployment insurance and other economic supports to get him through the ebbs and flows of construction work. The following ethical principle applies here:

Value: Social Justice (NASW, 2008)

Ethical Principle: Social workers challenge social injustice.

Social workers strive to ensure access to needed information, services, and resources; equality of opportunity; and meaningful participation in decision making for all people. (p. 3)

It is also important to recognize that advocacy skills are required in work with clients in recovery. Some may have been undereducated and/or incarcerated and as a result may experience more difficulties in finding employment.

The third ethical issue focuses on rising rental costs and security deposits brought about by urban gentrification. Since this issue seems to be impacting several group members, it poses long-term opportunity for Lucas to become involved in social action to support affordable housing in the community.

Value: Social Justice (NASW, 2008)

Ethical Principle: Social workers challenge social injustice.

Social workers pursue social change, particularly with and on behalf of vulnerable and oppressed individuals and groups of people. Social workers' social change efforts are focused primarily on issues of poverty, unemployment, discrimination, and other forms of social injustice. (p. 3)

CASE ILLUSTRATION 10.4

CLINICAL SOCIAL WORK SPECIALIZATION

Tonya, the client with schizophrenia, is more vulnerable at this time because of her father's death. Kendra has several concerns about her client that raise ethical questions.

The first ethical concern has to do with Tonya's self-determination and her ability to care for herself at this stressful time. Kendra must utilize knowledge of the disease of schizophrenia, as well as a consult from the treatment team to ensure that Tonya has the protections and supports required. The value Kendra is relying on is client self-determination (NASW, 2008).

1.02 Self-Determination (NASW, 2008)
Social workers respect and promote the right of clients to self determination and assist clients in their efforts to identify and clarify their goals. Social workers may limit clients' right to self determination when, in the social workers' professional judgment, clients' actions or potential actions pose a serious, foreseeable, and imminent risk to themselves or others. (p. 4)

Additionally, Kendra is using professional consultation in accordance with 2.05 Consultation as follows:

2.05 Consultation (NASW, 2008)
(a) Social workers should seek the advice and counsel of colleagues whenever such consultation is in the best interests of clients.
(b) Social workers should keep themselves informed about colleagues' areas of expertise and competencies. Social workers should seek consultation only from colleagues who have demonstrated knowledge, expertise, and competence related to the subject of the consultation. (p. 9)

Kendra is correctly seeking consultation from the professional treatment team involved with the client. She is demonstrating an advanced level of critical thinking and growth in competency attainment.

SUMMARY

This chapter has provided a framework for students' continued development of social work's nine competencies and related practice behaviors during the second year in a specialization-focused field placement. Two second-year process recordings demonstrated typical specializations to illustrate competency attainment and practice behaviors in a specialization, which you can use as models in your own practice. Field instruction excerpts have been presented that show the student–field instructor interaction related to each process recording and demonstrate what types of discussions you can expect in your field instruction meetings.

Additionally, the chapter considered ethical issues that relate to the two illustrative process recordings in the chapter. Ethical dilemmas in these process recordings were reviewed as they relate to the NASW *Code of Ethics* (NASW, 2008). You will consider this code of ethics and others as you practice in your specialization.

Chapter 11 describes particular issues of students in employment-based field placements.

Chapter 11

Employment and Field Placement at the Same Site

INTRODUCTION

Students who use their place of employment for field work must manage the process of securing the field placement in partnership with their school's field office and with their agency. This can become more complicated than you may expect; therefore, guidelines and direction to help you to work with your agency of employment and your school are provided in this chapter. In addition, common pitfalls and assumptions students make about the role of their agency in their education will be addressed in order to maximize students' use of their employment setting.

GUIDELINES FOR DEVELOPING A FIELD PLACEMENT WITHIN YOUR AGENCY OF EMPLOYMENT

Keep in mind that the purpose of field work is to develop social work competencies at the professional bachelor in social work (BSW) or master in social work (MSW) level. The skills you use as a professional social worker must be grounded in theory and professional values. You will have to demonstrate that your thinking processes about your interventions with clients have a firm foundation in social work. Although you are working somewhere in social services and are doing some sort of counseling, case management, criminal justice, substance abuse treatment, or foster care work, what you will do as a student and how you will make assessments will differ from others because of the knowledge, values, and critical thinking you bring to your client interactions. The purpose of a work–study field placement is to provide access to social work education to students who could not complete school without being employed. Not every MSW or BSW program has developed the resources and supports to permit students to complete a field placement at an employment site. Thus, you should raise these issues upon admission to a program to find out what their policies and resources permit.

This chapter will move you through the important steps you will have to take to develop a field placement at your job site and to be effective in this undertaking.

Plan Early for Field Work at Your Employing Agency

Guideline 1. Your agency as an employer is not required to provide you with a field placement. You must shape your outlook with this in mind, so you will have a better chance of effectively working to secure a placement.

CASE ILLUSTRATION 11.1

JOB CLASSIFICATION AS COUNSELOR IN A RESIDENTIAL TREATMENT PROGRAM FOR TEENS

Jenny's job classification is as a counselor to teens in a residential treatment program. From time to time, she has sessions with their parents. She informed her supervisor and program director that she was applying to a social work program, and they wrote letters of reference on her behalf. She was accepted. Although they are supportive of her goals, it is best for Jenny to approach her supervisor to ask if she can be reassigned to a different position within the agency so she can fulfill educational requirements. She would need them to find a spot where the agency's needs can be stretched so that she can have a field placement while still maintaining employment and an income. She must remember that they are not required to do this for her. In some situations, moving her around may be impossible due to client needs or funding source constraints. In order for a viable educational assignment to be developed for Jenny, many people in the agency will have to work on her behalf.

Therefore, having demonstrated dedication as an employee is advantageous. This involves seeking supervision, being collegial with others, and following instructions. Finally, many agencies will require her to have received an excellent evaluation from her job supervisor in order for this accommodation to be made.

CASE ILLUSTRATION 11.2

STAFF AT NURSING HOME JOINTLY DEVELOP FIELD PLACEMENT FOR STUDENT EMPLOYEE

A nursing home employee, Nela, has been providing case management for residents and reports to a social worker in the facility. She handles two floors of residents, half of whom have forms of dementia or chronic mental illness, and many of whom are Spanish speaking. Her job description required Spanish language skill. As a student, she wonders what potential there is to be moved from the dementia unit to a field work role counseling higher-functioning residents, especially since she is the only Spanish speaker. Although they are looking for another worker, no one has been hired yet.

These are the dilemmas a student faces when trying to obtain a field placement within an employing agency. Consider what the agency supervisor would have to do to effect a field placement in this case.

Several people must reconfigure several other staff members' jobs. This undoubtedly occurs in part through the goodwill of others in the agency. One program manager indicated, "Yes, move Nela to my floor. I have three residents she can do counseling with, who are verbal with involved family. Nela can do a monthly family group on Sundays." The manager noted that Nela cares about the residents, and she is pleased to help her education. Nela's direct supervisor had to figure out how to cover her current cases, particularly the Spanish speakers. Being creative, Nela's supervisor indicated her willingness to supervise a social work intern who can handle some of the clients. She and the student will cover Nela's clients so Nela can go to another floor part-time. Further arrangements were made on her behalf.

When this possibility was presented to Nela, she recognized the difficulties involved in developing this plan, even if it is not fully to her liking. She did not say, "I won't come in Sunday," even though she sings in a choir. She can ask if the family group can be set up after church or make a compromise. Nela is grateful to the people who were involved in helping her maintain a job while completing a field placement.

Discussion

Field placement at your employing agency requires agency staff responsible for student education to carve out an educational piece for you, transfer you, provide licensed MSW supervision, and continue to pay you—a tall order for an agency with an overworked staff.

Guideline 2. Confer with your school's field work department. The MSW and BSW programs that permit employment-based field placements will have policies and guidelines for you to follow. Usually there is someone in the field department who works with students to develop the employment-based field placement. Find out who this is, and begin the conversation.

Schools' field departments will inform students in writing about how to plan for field work. Where applicable, information about employment-based field work will be included. Do not bypass these communications—overlooking important communications is a major pitfall of students. Despite being flooded with daily e-mails and other communication, if it comes from the school, assume it is important.

You also have to know the policies of your agency. Some large agencies have strict policies about employed student field placements. In addition to passing probation, which is a universal requirement, many have an employment minimum of two or three years and a supervisor's positive work evaluation. Smaller institutions may have more flexibility about the required length of employment.

Developing a Field Placement That Meets School Standards

Guideline 3. A placement at your job should look like any other field placement. If the school asks for three full days per week of field work, keep in mind that the general criterion is that half of your time should be in direct practice with clients. The rest of the weekly time is for staff meetings, case conferences, field instruction, writing process recordings, and progress notes. Most likely the placement will require at least one evening per week to accommodate clients. Therefore, your flexibility is needed to configure your schedule around your education.

The clients you see will depend on your level in the BSW or MSW program. Senior-year BSW and first-year MSW students have generalist tasks with individual, group, family, and community work. Second-year students need assignments to match their specializations.

In order for a field placement at your job site to be accepted by your school, several criteria should be met. The following represent the range of many schools' requirements:

- Change of assignment: The field assignment should be different from what you have been doing in your job. Clients have to be changed so that you begin by learning social work engagement skills.
- Change of supervisor: A social worker with a license who meets the school's requirements may serve as field instructor.
- Distinct time for field work: If your field work in the nursing home is on a different floor from your job, designated continuous hours must be defined for the entire year of field placement. For example, you may be assigned to

field work on Mondays and Wednesdays from 8:00 a.m. to 1:00 p.m., Fridays from 9:00 a.m. to 5:00 p.m., plus four hours on Sunday afternoon. This adds up to 21 hours. Your job duties will be maintained with help from other staff. The four hours on Sunday comprise additional time after you have completed hours for your job. There was no other release time possible.

- No overlapping roles: A teacher may not serve as the social work intern at his or her employing school. A nurse in an outpatient psychiatric program may not be the social work intern in his or her same program. The student may be transferred to a mental health clinic with different clients under the title of "social work intern," not "nurse." Positions that are not part of social work departments pose more difficulty for students in obtaining field placements, since they were hired in another department. Therefore, designing a field placement for you may be an insurmountable challenge. Neither classroom nor patients can lose a teacher or nurse. Students who must maintain employment may work with the school for an off-hours field placement.

When faced with these scheduling limitations, taking classes after work and enrolling in a part-time program are most effective. A slower pace allows students to successfully complete field work. Seeking counsel from the field office will prove effective in your forward movement. Although hectic, this is manageable. Winter and spring breaks allow you to catch up on your numerous requirements. Midyear gives you a break from classes but not from field work, allowing extra time. Like those sleepless nights with a newborn that feel like they will last forever, those days pass. This situation is time limited.

Additionally, you must review your school's application for work–study placement. While each school's application is different, there are common elements that apply everywhere:

- Description of your current job and name of your current supervisor: This information will be required by your program in order to establish your current job duties and how the agency plans to change your workload.
- Description of your proposed student assignment: The agency's educational coordinator is usually responsible for developing your role for field work and writing it up for the school.
- Name of proposed field instructor and credentials: By the time this material is submitted to the school, there should be an agency MSW who has assumed the responsibility for providing weekly field instruction. He or she should meet the school's criteria, which include two to three years post MSW experience, a license, and involvement in any required training for field instructors.

- Several signatures: Usually more than one signature from the agency is required—that of the educational coordinator, field instructor, as well as your signature. This forges the agency and school in a relationship on behalf of your education.

COMMON PROBLEMS AND PITFALLS

Despite the many things that can go right in your placement in your place of employment, you may experience some challenges as well. These are outlined in the following sections.

Unlearning Prior Non-Social Work Roles

Students employed at their field placement site typically have pre-professional social work–related experience. In that role, you developed a sense of competency in working with clients' emotional and practical issues. While this helps you gain entry to a social work program, it is important that you are wary of feeling too competent. Your primary role now is that of social work student. This means embracing the self-concept of someone who does not know rather than that of someone who knows.

As a student, you will be subject to a level of supervision that you undoubtedly have not had before and assigned tasks with clients at a more complex level. The tasks you will undertake are in your student role as a person involved in coursework and social work supervision. The tasks will feel somewhat familiar. A common pitfall is when trying to feel comfortable on the job, the student may rush to apply known behaviors. Try to hold back when you are about to do that. The following case illustration demonstrates this common issue.

CASE ILLUSTRATION 11.3

EMPLOYED STUDENT IN A FOSTER CARE PROGRAM

Joanna, a social work student, has previously worked in a foster care program. In her job, she worked with foster parents and occasionally oversaw meetings between children and biological parents.

Her field placement is focused on family reunification. One biological mother, Carla, is a former crack addict who left her two children at home—ages 6 and 8—one night to go out and prostitute herself so that she could buy drugs. She has been clean for six months. In her meeting with Joanna, Carla discussed how she will find a job at Walmart or Costco. Joanna asked about her hourly wage. She said it is either minimum wage or a little more. Joanna asked how Carla will manage her finances in caring for two children. Carla said that food stamps and Medicaid will help her, and the children qualify for school lunches. Carla noted that with the children she also qualifies for public housing. She then asked if Joanna can help her obtain public housing since she has been in rehab and living in a treatment center. Joanna said she will help and cautioned that it will improve her chances if she has a job before she applies.

Later on in the meeting, Carla said she has been thinking about going back to school. Joanna said it is a good idea but suggested she consider how child care will work if she is working and going to school.

Supervision With Field Instructor

Manny is Joanna's field instructor. After having read the process recording, he said, "Let's look here where she tells you she is going to find a job at Walmart or Costco and you ask her how much she will be paid—what was that about?" Joanna said she was concerned that the children would not have the standard of life they now have in foster care. Manny said that perhaps being with their mother may trump standard of life. Joanna said she is not sure.

Manny asked Joanna about the public housing interaction. Joanna said she was trying to advise her on how to put together the best options. He asked Joanna what she thinks her role as Carla's counselor is. Joanna said she has done that with mothers before—she would give them their best options and advise them on that. He pointed out that that was no longer her role—that Joanna needed to explore more in depth with Carla. Joanna said she was confused. He asked her to role-play the mother with him as the social worker. She said she wants to apply for public housing. He said it is best to do it if you have a job and then asked how she was feeling. She said she felt disillusioned, like he didn't believe in her.

Manny asked her to review her reaction to Carla going back to school. Joanna said, "I thwarted her again." "What could you have said?" "It's great that you want to go to school."

Manny went on to ask how she feels about this biological mother. Joanna admitted she doesn't feel Carla is ready to have her kids back and does not trust she will take care of them. He asked for indicators. Joanna said she is like every other drug addict mother she has worked with. He said, "Joanna, that's a stereotype. How can you make the assessment person for person? That's a social work role—making accurate assessments based on data gathering and facts. Isn't there a positive survival core in this mother—the impetus to be with her kids and some recognition not only that she screwed up, but why?" Joanna said that she has heard Carla and it is genuine. So Manny asked, "If she is genuine, what else could you have said to her that was not about the wages?" Joanna said she could have encouraged and supported her job search. Manny agreed and added that she could have noted that people are promoted from such entry-level jobs—they are never dead end. Joanna agreed that she saw these as a dead end.

Time Pressures

Although many agencies genuinely want to help their employees continue their schooling while they are employed, some will find it hard to provide the necessary release time for the student to meet field work or job demands.

You may have to work more than a 35-hour week to accommodate your job and field work. You may have to work five short days so you can leave early each afternoon to go elsewhere for field work time. You will be challenged to work more efficiently while maintaining professionalism in both sites and roles.

Something has to give. Social life is usually suspended during this time. Less time is spent with family and other projects are dropped. Students who do not condense their schedules and prioritize what is important for the year may fail classes because they took too many—trying to complete a program in two years designed for non-working students.

Your Work Supervisor Wants to See Your Field Evaluation or Process Recordings

Your field evaluation and process recordings are confidential educational documents between you, the field instructor, educational coordinator, faculty advisor, and the school. These documents are for educational purposes—not for your job—and are not to be used for your job review. If you are asked for these documents, inform your advisor and/or the director of field instruction.

Withholding Information and Avoiding Issues

Field education is complex—far more complex than holding an agency job prior to attending social work school. Talk to your faculty field advisor. Bring issues to the field office. If you don't understand it, don't try to figure it out on your own. Do not try to solve problems on your own because you do not want to reveal certain issues. This is not a productive strategy.

CASE ILLUSTRATION 11.4

STUDENT WITHHOLDS IMPORTANT INFORMATION FROM THE SCHOOL ABOUT A JOB SITUATION

First-year student Arlene could not have a placement at her job because there were no social workers employed at the agency. She told the school that she had been in contact with an agency she knew through her job, and they would give her a placement. Since this was a long-standing placement setting, the school approved the placement and assigned her there. A month into field work, the agency offered her a job. She quit her original job and accepted the offer but never told the school. Three months later, she was fired because she did not pass probation; as a result, she lost her field placement.

The educational coordinator noted to the school that Arlene had been told to inform the school of the job offer so that the agency might submit paperwork. Arlene chose not to do so although opportunities were presented for her to do this.

Thinking she knew what she was doing, Arlene never discussed the risks involved in turning a job into a field placement before passing probation with the field office or her advisor. For these reasons, most schools will not permit placements in job sites if the student has not passed probation. She would have been advised to keep her job and continue the field placement at this site.

When Arlene lost her job, there was no available recourse for protecting the field placement because neither the faculty field advisor nor the school knew that she had been employed there. When the advisor visited the agency, they simply talked about the field placement, which was different from the job.

CASE ILLUSTRATION 11.5

STUDENT DISCLOSES IMPORTANT INFORMATION TO THE SCHOOL ABOUT A JOB ISSUE

Lenny was fired from his job in a residential treatment program for teens because of insubordination. The school came to that conclusion, although the agency is not

(Continued)

(Continued)

permitted to provide grounds for termination of employment. His faculty field advisor knew about his difficulty and had tried to help him keep his job so that he could complete field work at another site.

Lenny was doing reasonably well at the field placement in the agency clinic, and his field instructor was able to handle his difficulty in taking direction. Lenny was listening and learning, and with input from his field advisor, he was able to use the feedback to develop a good skill set. Thus, when his job was terminated in March, two months before he was to graduate, the field instructor and the agency agreed that his studentship would continue in this setting until the end of the semester since he was passing field work.

Discussion

The difference between the two illustrations demonstrates that Lenny was able to discuss the difficulties he was having on the job with his faculty field advisor. He recognized why he functioned more effectively with the field instructor as an authority figure but not with his boss at the residence. He found a way to develop his self-awareness, and although it was an economic blow to lose his job, the future looked bright because he would have a degree and could find a better position.

On the other hand, because Arlene chose not to bring her difficulties to anyone at the school, she was left with no safety net and no way to consider the ongoing difficulties she was having, which led to the negative outcome of her probation. She had no job, no field work, and while she could collect unemployment, future field placement looked uncertain. She was advised to seek the support of the university counseling office in order to process what had happened. She was given the chance to return the following year to begin field work again.

SUMMARY

The most important conclusion from this chapter is this: Field work at your place of employment is complex and cannot be managed by the student alone. It is vital for you to involve the school, follow their procedures, and make every accommodation you can at your agency to obtain a field placement within your job. You must inform and consult with your faculty field advisor and all the important supports the school provides you when you are in this vulnerable situation. To do otherwise is professionally self-defeating.

Chapter 12 contains information about managing relationships with clients and your field instructor and handling the various demands in your field work experience.

Part IV

I Feel Like Spaghetti—All Strung Out

Chapter 12

Managing Stressful Relationships and Demands

INTRODUCTION

Social work students may encounter a number of potential stressors during their time in field placement. They must manage the unfamiliar role relationships of student to client and student to field instructor. They will be called upon to address unrecognized personal issues that may impact their professional functioning. Along with that, family demands will impede upon the student. The sum total of these unfamiliar demands may cause unrelenting stress.

This chapter highlights issues you will encounter in your relationships during field placement and provides tools to help you cope.

MANAGING STRESSFUL RELATIONSHIPS WITH CLIENTS

There are bound to be clients who leave unforgettable marks on you as a student. These are the clients whose emotions you will bring home. Some emotions are feelings of success in helping while also realizing the relationship's importance to the client. Others come from clients you may not be able to mentally shake loose, where you feel a strained relationship or whom you feel unable to help.

Several types of stressful client relationships are considered.

Being New to the Student Role

One stressor is created by being new to the student role. While there is discomfort in the unknown, the newness of being a student can maximize your commitment and attachment to clients. As a result, your emerging skill in problem solving with and on behalf of your clients will be strengthened.

Clients' Stories

Another stressor comes from some clients' stories. Their stories will reawaken your own, bringing about discomfort while at the same time creating an opportunity for you to gain additional mastery over your situation. However, this new

---

CASE ILLUSTRATION 12.1

THE STUDENT'S FIRST LONG-TERM CLINICAL CLIENT

Adriana, a divorced 50-year-old student who comes from an upper-middle-class suburb, finds herself frequently thinking about and seeing the face of her young client. Now in her 20s, the client recently left an abusive relationship. When she was young, she was sexually abused by her father in their country of origin. This immigrant client has so many vulnerabilities that cause Adriana to wonder at the end of each session if she did enough to help her. Having rights in her country of origin was an impossibility for the client. Therefore, she is used to feeling powerless. She is also undereducated and requires continuous support to earn a GED so that she can compete in the job market and begin to build self-esteem. Through her persistent interventions and advocacy, Adriana had the client evaluated to determine what type of classes she needed.

Adriana's empathic connection and first-time clinical relationship with a client with multiple problems leave her susceptible to experiencing secondary trauma. Her field instructor is a seasoned and empathic clinician who is able to guide Adriana's expression of dismay and hurt for her client. The field instructor supports her efforts and holds back from making a judgment that Adriana is "overinvolved." Adriana encourages the client's attendance and helps her feel capable of doing what is required.

CASE ILLUSTRATION 12.2

A CLIENT'S STORY REAWAKENS YOUR OWN

A young first-year student, Tamar, found that providing supportive counseling to a Holocaust survivor stirred up her own family history. Her client described some events that she had not shared with anyone in her family. Tamar presented the empathic stance of a social worker, and this allowed the client to provide more details. Tamar was moved to tears. Her background and history allowed her to connect with the client's feelings, and her innate empathic awareness facilitated her understanding.

In her field instruction meeting with Vincent, Tamar talked about her own grandfather and the impact on her mother's life as the child of a Holocaust survivor. Vincent asked about the impact on Tamar's life, and she shared that her mother shielded her from her grandfather's stories. After hearing more about her family dynamic, Vincent told her that in his own professional life there have been particular client stories that stayed with him. He commented that they have to find each client's story. He noted this is the takeaway—to look for the story—and credited her ability to do that in the client session.

Tamar will remember his words. Her feeling of connection to the client was universalized and affirmed.

Discussion

This illustration shows the territory of the social worker. The recognition that it is a privilege to be given the client's story is what prepares you to be impacted by it. This becomes a way of reframing the stress. The client gives you the story so that you can use your best self and support to be of help.

self-awareness and reflection can facilitate a creative use of self, which deepens the relationship with the client.

Unfinished Business

The stress of feeling you have not done enough to help the client is created when the student takes in the client's story and its dilemma. Here, students will dwell on unfinished business rather than on accomplishments and clients' newfound strengths.

CASE ILLUSTRATION 12.3

THE STUDENT'S FEAR OF ABANDONING THE CLIENT

Imagine you are a second-year student who will be graduating shortly. The 11-year-old boy, Billy, you saw for play therapy was hardly verbal when you met him; now you will have to leave him. Not only will you be breaking the bond but you will be doing this with a child whose attachments are already fractured. You have been up nights worrying about Billy. You tell your classmates, and they urge you to discuss this with your field instructor. Finally, you let her know the extent of your concern about the child "who is under my skin." How will you help Billy cope with your leaving, and how will you deal as well? You discuss your ethical concerns as you consider the ending process. It is possible that the agency will offer you a job and you can continue seeing the child, which will alleviate your guilt and sadness. But for now, you have to cope with this ending.

After listening to your concerns, your field instructor says, "Billy will remain in you forever. Let him know that. It is about internalizing the object so that he can internalize you. There is reciprocity in the healthy internalization of the object. When the object is internalized, the child has a better chance of developing an enduring higher level of ego functioning. If that is the case, then as much as you will miss each other, the therapy has been good. You did what you were supposed to do. Nice job." At that moment, you think about how fortunate you are to have learned about object relations and ego psychology in your work with Billy and the complexities of applicable attachment theories.

Discussion

With the privilege of receiving the client's story and the ensuing relationship comes the subsequent anxieties the student can feel about abandoning an especially vulnerable client. Here, the student came to see that the depth in the relationship with the child served to strengthen the child's ability to sustain a bonded future connection.

Difficult Clients

Another type of stressful relationship is with the client whom the student is having trouble reaching—the one he or she believes is dissatisfied and might leave. At times, the student may secretly wish the client will leave so that the stress disappears but will feel guilty if it happens, so he or she tries hard not to chase the client away.

CASE ILLUSTRATION 12.4

THE COMPLAINING CLIENT

Background

The student, Marianne, is a mature bachelor in social work (BSW) senior, and her client is the mother of a 10-year-old girl with attention deficit/hyperactivity disorder (ADHD). The placement is at a school for special needs children. When the mother came to the school to complain about how they were not meeting her child's needs, Marianne was present, and she began to tell her story. The client seemed to like talking with Marianne and was assigned to her. As a 40-year-old with five children, Marianne demonstrated a great deal of empathy for her plight. Prior to finishing her undergraduate work, Marianne had a business with her husband selling toys on the Internet and to department stores. She never finished college, and now she is happy to be in school, using her understanding of family dynamics to help.

Process Recording Excerpt

Every time Felice meets me, she has something to complain about. I observe that she does not want to accept that her child has learning and behavioral issues, some of which I believe she exacerbates. I have not confronted her because my field instructor does not feel she is ready for it, and I am controlling myself. This client makes me feel like a divorced father having to handle an irrational ex-wife.

I try hard to be empathic with her. For example, in this last session, she started to discuss how one public school didn't notice when a child with a disability left the school and eventually he was found wandering. She then asks exactly how security works in this school. I painstakingly explain it to her. I tell her what she already knows—that the security here is tested again and again and they have brought in consulting experts to ensure that it works. I invite her to talk to the security people.

However, it pops into my head from a discussion with my field instructor about her helplessness, and I say to Felice, "It must feel so helpless that you cannot make your child's ADHD go away." This stops her dead in her tracks, and she answers, "Yes, it is awful." I sit with the silence, and then I say, "You have done a good job bringing her here. She is doing so well." She goes on to say that it still doesn't take the feelings away. We talk more about how the kids have a community with each other and that adults with ADHD go on to function well. For the first time, I see that she lets herself understand that. And we go on to talk more about her issues with her child.

(Continued)

(Continued)

"I know how you feel. As a parent, I worry about the things that I cannot make right for my kids." I affirm that this is an unexpected blow that was thrown to the family and a challenge to her parenting.

I then ask, "What about your other children?" She says, "I don't worry about them." I ask why not, and she says they do well in school. So then I ask how they get along with Tara, and she says they are pretty good with her. I follow my perception that she is too preoccupied with Tara and not attentive to the others. "How are they doing beyond school?" I ask. "Okay. But it's Tara who has the problem." I say, "I'd like to hear about your other kids. Tara is doing okay. You know she has made great progress here. Tell me about the others." She went on to talk about her older son and daughter.

If I had not gotten her to express how helpless she feels, I never would have seen that we were accomplishing anything. She was unnerving to me. My field instructor listened to my complaints every time and just encouraged me to continue seeing her. I felt as though it was a message about my ethical responsibility to see people even if I did not like them. I understood and kept on. But once I made it okay for her to help her other children, she was like a changed person in the session.

Discussion

The breakthrough in this session is partly attributed to Marianne's ability to keep her field instructor's comments in the back of her mind. She used one comment directly to help the client recognize what she had been paying no attention to—that the child was doing well in the program. This allowed Marianne to focus discussion on the client's other children who also needed her attention. This change occurred because Marianne sought to treat the client fairly despite her ambivalent feelings about the complaining behavior.

MANAGING STRESSFUL RELATIONSHIPS WITH YOUR FIELD INSTRUCTOR

Another type of stress-producing relationship is the one with your field instructor. Inherent in it is your vulnerability in the role. What allows vulnerability is the service to clients. Students enter a social work program to learn how to help others. The altruistic driving force and the desire to learn propel the student's relationship with the field instructor.

To practice ethically, you have to present all your flaws and missteps about your client relationships with truthfulness to your field instructor. Sometimes you do not want the challenge. Other times you pursue the learning process.

There are several typical stressful factors in the student–field instructor relationship.

Field Instructor's Authority

One key stressor in the relationship with the field instructor is the fact that he or she has authority over the student. The field instructor prepares the student's evaluations and, to a large degree, determines how well the student is performing. The difficulty or ease with which a student handles the authority relationship is interactional. A student's shortcoming or unique characteristic combined with the field instructor's own teaching style and personality will create the relationship.

This type of relationship may be more challenging for the older student who came to school after having been competent elsewhere—the student who has forgotten what it was like to take classes and to be judged. Students who come straight from undergraduate school may deal more easily with education-related authority figures. Lacking certain life experiences, they conjure up empathy using history, family, and the arts to understand and may be more adaptable in being dependent on a field instructor who will be evaluating them. Others with a history of conflicted relationships with authority may also have difficulty being scrutinized and evaluated.

Parallel Process

Further complexity in the student–field instructor relationship arises out of what is called the "parallel process." A parallel process is created by a field instructor when the student–field instructor relationship replicates a dynamic in a student–client relationship (Williams, 1997). If planned by the field instructor, this helps the student internalize a way to interact with the client that is modeled within the latent process the student has with the field instructor. This is a unique aspect of clinical supervision not readily discussed as part of the student's learning experience (Shulman, 2006). However, parallel process is always part of the field instruction relationship.

For example, in Marianne's case, the field instructor tells Marianne to listen and stay with the complaining client but not to confront her. Marianne has been complaining to the field instructor about how this client annoys her, because she complains that her child's program is not up to her standard. The complaint underlies something else. However, the field instructor recognizes that Marianne is doing what the client is doing—complaining. The field instructor remains supportive of Marianne while cautioning her to be supportive of the client, not confrontational. This enables Marianne to continue to support the client, who eventually opens up because she posed an empathic statement. That is parallel process being used effectively.

Negative Parallel Process

Consider the situation of a student being harshly viewed by a field instructor. It is important that the student does not view his or her own clients harshly—that is, the student should not replicate the negative parallel process. You may be familiar with this type of negative parallel process in harsh organizational settings where the leadership is punitive and the managers become punitive to their direct reports. When a student in this dilemma has the self-reflection required to bring the issue to the faculty field advisor's attention, a solution may ensue. The student may receive support, not harsh treatment, which helps to preserve the positive role with clients.

CASE ILLUSTRATION 12.5

I NEVER SEEM TO BE ABLE TO PLEASE MY FIELD INSTRUCTOR

Melissa was placed at a high school and has a field instructor who she feels is harsh. She is a young student with a tendency to be fearful of people in authority. In her first-year field placement, she had some problems taking direction from her field instructor, who was kind, astute, and supportive. Her faculty field advisor that year recommended she obtain counseling and she did. In working with grandparents in the kinship foster care program, she came to understand their problems having to discipline children exhibiting conduct issues in school. Her own therapy helped her adapt to the requirements of the placement and to the field instructor's feedback. She developed skills, wrote process recordings, and her field instructor and faculty advisor helped her to grow. Melissa does not like the bureaucratic structures of school systems but likes the idea of working with teens. She has the ability to engage young people and to be effective with them.

Her current field instructor told the faculty field advisor, Dr. Reynolds, that Melissa is distant from the school's professional staff. In meeting with Dr. Reynolds, Melissa reported that the field instructor does not like her and that she has been trying to make it work by spending time with the children and writing process recordings. Admittedly, she is not overly friendly toward or engaging with her field instructor except during their sessions. She noted that the field instructor does not read her process recordings and says that the reverse is true, that her field instructor avoids her.

Knowing that he could not share details of his conversation with Melissa, Dr. Reynolds intervened with the field instructor on Melissa's behalf. He suggested that the field instructor rely on the strengths' perspective with Melissa by focusing on her positive attributes rather than her perceived limitations. He asked for the field instructor's view of Melissa's process recordings. The answer was vague, and he did not ask further. This sent a message to the field instructor that she was expected to read them.

Melissa and Dr. Reynolds discussed moving her from the placement. There was no other option to change her field instructor at the high school. The unsuccessful struggle to please a field instructor created a bind for Melissa, who did not want to relinquish her relationships with the children. Thus, she decided to remain at the placement and to sidestep being drawn into a negative parallel process by making the children feel they could never please her.

Experiencing Practice Issues

Students will feel stressed when they are not meeting demands or when they feel in conflict with the field instructor. The stressful relational situation escalates when a student is having serious practice issues and does not work on the issues because he or she does not accept or reflect on the field instructor's feedback and assessment. At this point, the student and field instructor are at an impasse. The faculty field advisor usually becomes involved in presenting the problem to the student and providing an additional learning contract.

If you find that you have questions about feedback from your field instructor, bring them to your faculty field advisor. The field instructor constructs the educational assessment and evaluates your progress in the field. The student and the field instructor are not equals in this relationship. It is essential to avoid an adversarial "I am right, she is wrong" relationship. Thus, disputes with a field instructor's assessment should be brought to the school for additional review and feedback.

Other Relationship Issues

Students will feel added stress when the field instructor is not meeting the school's or the student's demands. A good drill for becoming a professional is to realize that the only aspect of the relationship that is in your control is you.

CASE ILLUSTRATION 12.6

MY FIELD INSTRUCTOR MEETS WITH ME, BUT DID NOT WRITE MY EVALUATION

William has a field instructor who meets with him regularly to review his work. The agency works with people with behavioral health issues. He has received useful feedback and learned a great deal from his field instructor. However, it is well into the second semester, and she has not submitted his first semester evaluation. William discussed this with his faculty field advisor. He feels somewhat cheated because he wants to know exactly what he needs to improve in developing social work competencies.

The field office maintains the evaluation records and the director of field work asked the advisor to follow up with the field instructor. William has sought out the field director on two occasions to express his frustration. In William's presence, the field director informed the agency educational coordinator that the evaluation was long overdue. The educational coordinator immediately sent an e-mail to the field instructor, copying the field director. The school did what they were supposed to do. The faculty field advisor compensated by giving feedback to William about what he saw as his strong skill set and what he needed to work on in the remaining time.

Discussion
William handled himself well because he did not let this situation interfere with his relationship with the field instructor. His sense of roles, responsibilities, and even limitations in the real world sustained him.

MANAGING ISSUES AT THE AGENCY

A third stress-producing relationship occurs at the agency. There are a number of issues that may arise—some that you can control and others that you cannot.

Compliance Issues

Another problematic aspect of the relationship with a field instructor and other agency staff that creates stress for the student is more about compliance and less about the student's practice. The focus is on the student's reliability in meeting agency tasks, as well as timeliness and attendance. Progress notes, process recordings, and psychosocial assessments must be submitted on time, and clients have to be seen as scheduled. When a student does not meet these requirements, he or she is responsible for creating this stress, not the field instructor. This also causes strain in the student's relationship with the field instructor. Field instructors do not want to oversee the student's completion of tasks.

The following illustration shows how a student managed some of her requirements but not all of them and the implications for becoming employed in that setting.

CASE ILLUSTRATION 12.7

SECOND-YEAR STUDENT IS PLACED IN AN URBAN MEDICAL CENTER

Nora is placed in a large Midwestern urban hospital. Before she accepted the placement, the field director asked if she could manage the pressures and time constraints of this setting, given her child care issues. She was asked to weigh the options and give her answer the following week. The director assured her there were other settings that would be less demanding. The placement carried a stipend, and that is the reason the field director even discussed this with her.

Rounds happen at 8:30 a.m., and there have been occasions when Nora has been late. The director of social work has taken note, and while it has been mentioned by the field instructor, her lateness has not been focused on to avoid demoralizing an otherwise reasonably capable student. There are times when Nora submits her process recordings late as well. The educational coordinator and other staff have said informally that a medical setting does not tolerate lateness and let it be known that a student who shows any time management issues will never be hired.

Nora has heard this message and has been encouraged by her field instructor to seek positions with more flexibility once she graduates.

Discussion

What should be understood is that while Nora's field instructor finds her to be capable, this agency would not find her suitable as an employee or colleague. Had she overstepped her time management issues further, she would have been asked to leave the placement. Fortunately, Nora managed to hang on. Students should know that if they wish to be considered for employment at their field placement they should have no time management issues.

Unexpected Issues

Neither the student, nor the school, nor the agency planned the change. But as the pre-Socratic Greek philosopher, Heraclitus said, "You cannot step twice into the same river" (Burnet, 1892). Your field placement agency was reorganized, and staff were let go. Your field instructor is still working; therefore, you are still there. Perhaps your whole unit was moved to another location, creating a longer commute for you. These changes impact staff and they impact clients. Whenever changes occur, you will have to show flexibility and adaptability.

When Hurricane Katrina hit in August 2005, the students at Tulane University School of Social Work had to stop their education just as it was about to begin. The university closed for one semester, and the dean of the social work school arranged for other programs around the country to take the students and provide them with placements (S. R. Gelman, dean of Wurzweiler School of Social Work [WSSW], personal communication, September 2005). This was accomplished under difficult circumstances. But the students returned with many having completed field placements. All graduated with degrees from Tulane.

In the northeast, Hurricane Sandy rendered many students who lived or were placed in surrounding areas either homeless, without electricity, or with forced field site relocation. A treatment program for mentally ill clients was closed for six weeks. Therefore, a program's second-year student helped hurricane victims in her community, using social work skills to bring resources to them. Another student herself was relocated from a flooded high rise on the beach to public housing downtown, to another placement, and her child moved to another school. One student, who had been resistant about doing a partial placement in an assemblyman's office, ended up providing an important service to constituents in the neighborhood, which heightened his self-esteem and enriched his ability to help. Still another student, initially fearful that she did not have the skills to help all the people at her placement who had been displaced, pulled herself together with, "I have to. I am needed." Students adapt to their situations and do all kinds of wonderful things.

Students in California have dealt with local disasters. During the Rodney King race riots in 1992, graduate master in social work (MSW) students provided crisis support to the community through an intervention conceived and supervised by several faculty and the dean. This was conducted through public television's fund-raising phone bank that was used to handle crisis calls (J. Nunn & M. Maki, personal communication, 1992), with students speaking with local residents afraid to go out. The students were ethnically and racially mixed and through intense supervision and debriefing handled the challenges and biases of the callers.

During a crisis related to 9/11, an entire clinic operation was moved from the Ground Zero area to outer boroughs, and students traveled far to provide support for mentally ill clients (K. Zuckerman, personal communication, 2001). Incidentally, September 11, 2001, was the second day of field work for all New York schools of social work.

Events happen, and the river flows unpredictably. Crises should be expected that are beyond the individual situations that clients bring to your meetings.

When a student's field instructor is let go, this is usually a terrible loss for the student. The school, through the assistance of the faculty field advisor and the field director, will help the student cope with this change and will work with the agency to provide alternative field instruction.

Agency Issues

Other agency occurrences may include labor disputes, job actions, and strikes. Agency managers plan in advance for how they will work with clients in the event unionized staff will stage a strike or job action. Although they may know about the advanced planning, most schools' policies dictate that students are not to go to field placement or to become involved in labor disputes or strikes. If a labor dispute or strike occurs at your agency, you must speak with your field advisor and field director right away and seek support and advice. Any disruptions and changes that are about to happen must be brought to the school's attention.

Plans will be made by the school for making up hours missed in field work during that time. If strikes become prolonged, schools will usually arrange for students to be placed elsewhere. Although strikes create upheaval in targeted areas, other local agencies will help the schools involved and support their students by providing alternative field placements for them.

MANAGING DEMANDS OF FAMILY AND FRIENDS

Consider the multiple roles you handle in your life and who the members of your role set are. You are a wife, father, daughter-in-law, brother, employee, friend, choir leader, or rabbi. Every one of these relationships and activities will have to be curtailed in some creative way for the time being.

Relationships and Activities

Prioritizing what is most important in your life—what is necessary, and what can be postponed or rearranged—is a useful approach. You will not be able to meet all of everyone else's demands. It is flawed thinking to believe you can do everything. Social work school requires that you do everything in the program well. The shortcut of ordering takeout for the family dinner has no counterpart in the classroom. The paper has to be written well, whereas the meal does not even have to be cooked. Arranging for others to handle Thanksgiving this year is a good idea. This allows you to devote your time to field work, classes, and to be attentive rather than preoccupied. In reconfiguring tasks, new leadership may develop at home.

The pitfalls students have to guard against include people in their lives who make them feel bad when they have less time for them. The pressure they exert may undermine the student's forward movement. "You are always writing a paper. Come to the guys' night out. We never see you anymore." "We are doing a girls' day at the spa. Where are you?" You are trying to get some sleep so that you will worry less and be clearheaded enough to think through how to handle your termination with the 11-year-old with an attachment disorder.

There are also people who do not understand or accept what you are doing. They may say, "What do you think a social worker can do that a friend can't? Someone who talks to a social worker must have no friends." Or they make statements like, "Why do you want to help people who are drug addicts? They did this to themselves."

These messages should cause the student to evaluate his or her relationships with the messenger. Reviewing how and if to approach the people who present negativity about your goals rather than support them is helpful. It may be a good idea to reappraise those relationships with people who do not help or support your advancement. It also may involve becoming more realistic about what can be expected from particular people.

CASE ILLUSTRATION 12.8

SECOND-YEAR STUDENT WHO WOULD LIKE TO COUNT ON HELP FROM HER MOTHER

Vanessa is a 45-year-old single mother. Her mother has not been very helpful with her children as she spends over half of her time in another state. Vanessa is divorced from an abusing husband whom her mother did not encourage her to leave. She feels that every move she has made to advance her life has been subtly prevented by her mother, who herself has difficulty changing the status quo. Now Vanessa needs her mother because she is having surgery. She has to rely upon her to come back to town and stay with her children for two weeks while she recovers. She is having this done during the school's spring break while the children are home so that she will not miss her class and field work. She is not optimistic that her mother will help, and it hurts her that she has to beg for support. After some therapy, she has come to be more forgiving and less needy. However, anger arises at those times when she feels other mothers would come to their adult children's aid.

Her mother offered to have the children at her winter home in the Southwest. Vanessa is reluctant to disrupt their routine and take them away from their friends. She would prefer her mother to come to her house and help supervise their comings and goings and activities during this time.

Discussion

Vanessa feels trapped and unsupported. Perhaps she has other options. First her supports should be reviewed to consider who else can be counted on. Given that she has managed school by herself up until now, she undoubtedly has more supports than she realizes. The possibility exists that the children have friends they can be with during this time. During holidays, children enjoy the chance to be with others so they can solidify their friendships. Activities can be arranged for them that rely on other parents, rather than involving her mother. However, Vanessa will have to continue to let go of her wish that her mother will be available to meet her needs.

CASE ILLUSTRATION 12.9

SECOND-YEAR MARRIED STUDENT DEALING WITH FAMILY DEMANDS

Zeke is a 27-year-old student. He married right after college, and while he is in social work school, his wife, Jeanette, has been supporting them financially. After he graduates, they are planning to start a family. Jeanette does not like her job. She works in an accounting firm as a support staff, and although she did not finish college, she is being paid well. She complains frequently that Zeke is still in school and how much she wants to leave her job. This creates undue pressure and guilt on Zeke. He would prefer that she return to college, even while he is in school, complete her degree, and then they can start a family. Her mother pressures her to have a child.

Discussion

Zeke's options appear to be minimal, but they are not. However, the issues presented have to be partialized and prioritized. The situation with his wife is time limited. Once he completes his degree, he will be able to find employment. This will

(Continued)

(Continued)

please them both. This might be the first topic to discuss to raise her morale and alleviate his guilt.

The second issue revolves around what should happen once Zeke completes his degree. Should they start a family? He would prefer his wife finish college first— even to go back to college now. However, Zeke's agenda has to be discussed with her and should be viewed against her own agenda of starting a family. There may be another underlying factor—his mother-in-law's agenda for her daughter: that she have a child sooner rather than later. However, she may be mirroring her daughter's wishes rather than pressuring her. This is the second area for discussion between Zeke and Jeanette.

SUMMARY

Many students feel like spaghetti at this point. Sometimes you have to cut the spaghetti; otherwise you will be entangled in it and it won't fit in your mouth. Other times you have to get rid of half of it to wrap it around your fork.

This chapter has focused on the stressful relationships students experience in the professional sphere with clients and field instructors. Everything you do in social work school requires reflection so that you may integrate theory with practice to accept clients' stories and your own vulnerability. The desire to be effective with clients pushes your productive engagement in field instruction despite whatever conflicts or uncertainties are experienced in the relationship. This chapter also focused on the stressful relationships students experience in the personal sphere with family and friends. Knowing that compromises have to be made and certain obligations with family and friends have to be temporarily neglected is important for your success in your program. Understanding the differences between support and lack of support from family and friends is also necessary.

Chapter 13 addresses the self-awareness issues students must cope with, which include the impact of personal history on practice.

Chapter 13

Utilizing Self-Awareness in Social Work Practice

INTRODUCTION

Participating in field placement challenges the student to recognize and address personal historical issues and their impact on the student's work with clients. It is impossible for a student to practice effectively or ethically with clients without having examined his or her personal issues. It is important to be aware that students' resistances to looking at these issues may create conflict with their field instructors and faculty field advisors.

This chapter highlights how your personal history can be used productively to enhance your practice. It also examines how some personal issues become impediments to effective practice. Approaches are offered to overcome the pitfalls and minefields that unresolved personal issues can pose. Guidelines are provided for managing your own issues in the field work context. Through illustrations, further strategies are highlighted for dealing with persistent issues that threaten your professional functioning. The Johari Window (Luft & Ingham, 1955) is used to illuminate a six-step process to enhance your personal understanding.

USING YOUR HISTORY AND ISSUES TO ENHANCE YOUR WORK

The aspiration to become a social worker is usually brought about by an element in a student's personal history that compels him or her to make this career choice. This history is usually comprised of life-altering events that have created a deepened empathy and sensitivity to particular circumstances. These events enable identification with a client's plight or predicament. Along with identification and empathy, there is the desire to gain professional tools to help others as the student has been helped. The major theme is the conviction that your learning can be used to benefit someone else in similar circumstances. Others have found you to be a good listener and a trustworthy helpful friend.

For example, a student may have experienced the early death of a friend, which heightened his understanding of loss and transformed his life's purpose. Another student may have lived through her mother's abuse by a significant other. The mother's ability to escape was the life forming circumstance that motivated her desire to help other women. One student entered social work school after her child died of a long illness. Prior to accepting her for field work, a team of staff conducted interviews to determine if her personal loss had been resolved to the degree required for her to be empathic yet maintain boundaries. Some students previously received mental health treatment from social workers; this becomes the foundation of their commitment to helping.

Other students who have been members of church, synagogue, community action, and youth organizations transfer that involvement to social work school. The experience of trauma and victimization or the stigma of disability has created in some students a strong sense of justice and altruism that has brought them to a social work program.

To better understand what is behind your commitment to being a social work student, several steps are outlined to direct your self-awareness in your work with clients.

Step 1: Identify Your Personal Interest in Social Work

Consider whether the motivation that brought you to the social work program comes primarily from a broader altruism, from personal history, or both. All motivations have legitimacy. Understanding the elements of your motivation requires you to pause and reflect in order to tell your story. Telling it to yourself and writing it down provides clarity and brings your story into view. Shedding light on your inspirations for choosing social work will help you to use them effectively.

Step 2: Use the Johari Window—Quadrants I and II

Once you have expressed the words that are associated with your application to a social work program, you are ready to examine them closely. Begin the examination by constructing a Johari Window (Luft & Ingham, 1955) of four empty quadrants.

In Quadrant I (aspects of self that are *known to self and known to others*), fill in what inspired you to become a social worker—that particular aspect of your inspiration that is known to you and to others. These are the themes in your application to the social work program and the narrative you told in your face-to-face interview.

In Quadrant II (aspects of self that are *known to self and unknown to others*), write those parts of the story that are only known to you but not generally known to others. This is what you did not tell your interviewers or may not have expressed in your personal essay. For example, the fact that you were bullied is known to others and to you. However, others do not know that you were sexually assaulted in high school. Write these down; you can even write them in code to protect yourself.

The student who understands how these issues impacted herself or himself is able to work with clients. The following case illustration demonstrates what this looks like.

Figure 13.1   Johari Window

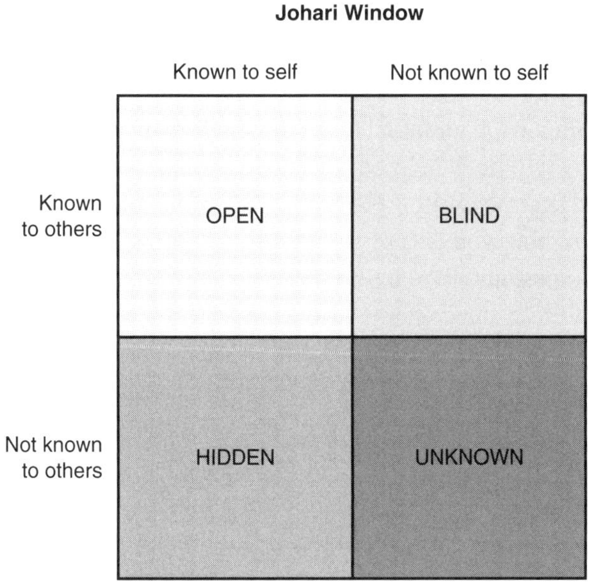

Source: Luft, Joseph (1999). The Johari Window: A Graphic Model of Awareness in Interpersonal Relations. In Cooke, Alfred L., Brazzel, M., Saunders Craig, A., and Greig, B., (Ed.), *The Reading Book for Human Relations Training, 8th Edition* (pp. 51–54). Silver Spring, MD: NTL Institute for Applied Behavioral Science.

CASE ILLUSTRATION 13.1

STUDENT IN MIDDLE SCHOOL GROUP—BULLYING ISSUE

Liz, a first-year student, has a field placement in a middle school. She knows that bullying is an important issue to work on with the kids. In one of her groups, she discussed bullying by exploring with members which "types of kids they don't usually hang out with." Her field instructor said that she is engaging them well and credited her ability to understand the various cliques in the school. Eventually the youngsters came to see that the members of this group may not be the types of kids they would usually choose to hang out with. She used this awareness to help them to become more inclusive outside of the group and to accept those who are different from them. Liz believes that when they recognize and understand the differences they are less likely to bully and to be bullied.

As a result of her own, more hidden experiences, Liz tries to pay attention to any potential for sexual assault and the possibility that victimization may be happening in the children's lives outside of school.

She is confident that her own experiences have helped her understanding.

Step 3: Continue the Johari Window—Quadrant III

When turning to Quadrant III (aspects of self that are *unknown to self and known to others*), you will need help because the items are unknown to you. The contents of Quadrant III are based on the feedback you receive in the learning process in field work and how you accept it. The more feedback you accept, the smaller the quadrant becomes, and the larger Quadrant 1 becomes.

In order to fill in the contents of Quadrant III, consider what your field instructor has said to you about your work. Although you are doing well with your group, some feedback may have come in the form of a question about interventions that you have bypassed. Reflecting upon the question or comment shows you the unknown items in Quadrant III. In those exchanges, your field instructor is guiding you to an understanding you have not yet attained. Say that your field instructor commented, "I see that Henry told the group that he wished he could get more hits in his Little League baseball game. You then asked if he was being made fun of for not hitting. He said that he wasn't. You did not go further. Is there anything else that could be going on besides bullying that you could have addressed?"

The issue your field instructor raised has not been revisited. Thus, in Quadrant III, you should write down that you were stuck on bullying as a theme and missed the

Figure 13.2   Johari Window—Personal Feedback Tool

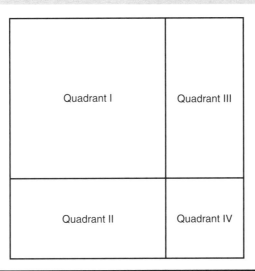

fact that Henry may have been requesting a hitting lesson. This comment gives you an opening to discuss how the group can approach not knowing or having the skills to do something. In this process, you begin to see that your vision may become clouded based on your own personal history. Everything is not about bullying.

If you are able to return to Quadrant III to retrieve those items that you avoided, then you are on the path to self-correction and learning. However, this will not always happen, and you may find your personal issues obstructing your work.

WHEN YOUR PERSONAL ISSUES GET IN THE WAY

Your personal issues are getting in the way when you deflect the feedback being given. One sign that personal issues are interfering is when a student begins feeling picked on by his or her field instructor. The student becomes argumentative and creates a conflictual relationship, an unfortunate approach since the field instructor has to be seen as the expert, while the student is not.

If you find yourself in this mode with a field instructor, pause and consider. These reactions may be signs that you are avoiding a piece of self-reflection. Although field instructors are not perfect, listening is more effective than reacting. If you are stuck, find a peer at school who will be honest with you, and talk it through. You may ask your faculty field advisor for input. Reviewing the feedback with your field instructor is the ultimate goal. If the impasse continues, it is useful to talk with the field director at your school. And finally, it may be useful to seek help from your school's counseling office.

Step 4: Identify Your Self-Awareness Issues

It is important for the well-being of your clients that you understand your personal issues and impediments. The following are some common self-awareness problems that are unknown to self but known to others, which will limit your role with clients.

Lacking Depth

One major problem of students is the inability to accept that they are having educational issues in the field. For example, your field instructor tells you that your presentation of an interaction with your client did not demonstrate the depth required of a second-year student. Rather than reflecting, you become reactive, saying that you do not understand what she means.

Lacking depth means the student did not use any theories to understand the client or to guide or review his or her interventions. Applying theory to your interactions with clients and then reflecting on the interactions is a competency you must have after the foundation year and that you will build upon in the second year. Lacking depth usually means that the student discussed the client interaction superficially and not as a social worker. The parallel would be if the student reported elbow pain to a doctor and the doctor didn't provide a technical description of possible causes of the pain or ask questions to find its origin and consider treatments.

Lacking depth also indicates that the student likely did not read the professional literature that provides the depth required. Thus, critical thinking in the application of theory was not used. This student appears to be trying to slide by. Reading these books or articles will provide the depth required.

Where Are YOU in the Process?

A field instructor tells a student that the student is missing from the process recording. The student has met with the wife of a man arrested for possession of a small amount of marijuana. From her placement in the public defender's office the student knows this is a minor offense. The field instructor does not see the student's empathy for the wife in the process recordings or in their supervisory meeting. In field instruction the student reports that the wife is raising the couple's 2-year-old and 6-month-old and is afraid that if her husband is incarcerated, she will end up on welfare. The student does not show the ability to explore the client's feelings. The field instructor asks the student how the client is feeling. She does not know but supposes that the client has much on her plate and is worried. The field instructor asks, "How can you find out?" The student replies, "I can ask."

The field instructor is aware that the student performs well as an advocate and a problem solver but has a hard time listening. She will have to review the process recording and reflect on her role with the client to consider what the client's feelings were and how she did or did not respond. It is important that the student does not gloss over the field instructor's words and questions. Rather, using the feedback to consider more effective approaches is essential.

Personal Issues in Your Unique History

Students' personal issues and their impact on student–client relationships must be examined. While always present, several key issues surface at times when clients' issues are replicating those of the student.

CASE ILLUSTRATION 13.2

AFRICAN AMERICAN STUDENT WHO GREW UP IN A HIGH-RISK COMMUNITY

Jake is African American, and he grew up in the projects. He feels very fortunate that he was not swallowed up by the area. Around him were many young teens who dropped out of school and were lost to drugs and gangs. He understands that some of their parents were lost too, which made it hard for them to see a better future. Jake has openly said, "I narrowly escaped with my life. While people dropped out, neither my parents nor siblings were lost to the streets. I received many benefits for being a good student. With scholarships, loans, and a job, I graduated from a local college. I went into AmeriCorps, which gave me the impetus to enter social work school. Despite having some hard times, we all persevered."

Discussion

Jake's background makes him a good candidate for social work school. He found his way to a service program for college graduates—a perfect segue into a social work master's degree.

Jake will have to be aware that in his field placement with youth offenders, his desire for them to finish high school and go on to college does not override his understanding of what they want. While he has had access to a high-quality education, in making assessments of his clients, he must be wary of superimposing his wants on them. Alternative or vocational education may be within his clients' view. At the same time, he also has to become their advocate when the system sets low expectations. He will have to fiercely expand their aspirations while at the same time separating himself from his own agendas for them.

CASE ILLUSTRATION 13.3

STUDENT WHO WAS RAISED AS A FOSTER CHILD

Rosie attended the same school as Jake. However, she was in foster care. Her mother, a drug addict, contracted AIDS and died while Rosie was in high school. Rosie made it to college with the support of her teachers and therapists. The relationship with her foster family was complicated because her two foster brothers were not college bound, and as the only high achiever in the household, she often felt alone. Rosie chose social work because she wanted to help in the same way she had been helped.

Step 5: Consider the Extent to Which Your Self-Awareness Issues Are Resolved

Perhaps, if you are like Jake, in believing you worked hard to make a good life for yourself, you have become judgmental of those who ended up in gangs or in prison. Your challenge will be to suspend your judgments about what should have been. It will be necessary to follow your field instructor's lead when you are asked how your own life story colors your view of the client. Concluding that you are not experiencing a reaction should give you pause.

Rosie, believing that the foster care system is not helping her client, does not hear her field instructor's direction on how to work with the foster family. If you are making decisions that are not within the realm of your field instructor's guidance, you may be trying to do it your way. Since you are a student, it should not be possible to do it your way. Continuing on this path is going off the deep end without a life jacket. Your field instructor is the life jacket. Get out before sinking, and return to your field instructor to figure out what to do next. Then take the time to reflect on why you were trying to do it your way.

CASE ILLUSTRATION 13.4

SECOND-YEAR STUDENT'S UNRECOGNIZED SELF-AWARENESS ISSUE

Sandy, a second-year student, is placed in a mental health treatment program for people with HIV. She holds back in her interactions with clients, and her presentation with her field instructor has been guarded throughout her first semester. Her field instructor reported that she is uncooperative and does not follow through on directions related to clients. Sandy said that she stays late at the agency to write in the charts and that she is hard working. Her process recordings reflect connections with her clients, while showing her inability to recognize latent content that would enhance a more clinical sustaining relationship.

In her process recording, Sandy wrote that the client says she is frightened by her father. Sandy responded in a superficial manner. In her supervision, Sandy resisted this interpretation by her field instructor. Her lack of response is revisited, this time by her faculty field advisor who challenges her to consider why she did not pick up on what the client said. Sandy claimed she has no idea. Her advisor asked if any of the client's issues bear resemblance to her own family history. Sandy responded that they do not. Her advisor asked further, "What was your family like?" Sandy described a strict West Indian upbringing with a father who worked hard. When her advisor asked how she felt about him, Sandy admitted to being afraid. Upon further discussion, Sandy revealed that her mother protected her interests better than her father. Eventually, she admitted that her father had been abusive with her and that she feared him.

A key reason why Sandy was able to hear her faculty field advisor is because they developed a trusting relationship. In addition, she wants to succeed in the master in social work (MSW) program. Her guardedness was pointed out to her, and to her credit, Sandy allowed her advisor to cut through her defensiveness. After a lengthy meeting that can best be described as an educational crisis intervention session, Sandy came to understand the implications of her own denial and decided to seek the services of university counseling. She was given a different placement that is more focused on case management.

Step 6: Revisiting the Johari Window—Quadrant III

Having considered common self-awareness issues, it is useful to now reconsider the Johari Window. With all that you have seen about yourself, you may decipher those issues that are unknown to you and known to others that have been eluding you. Include them in Quadrant III so that you may expand your self-awareness.

In following this step in the exercise, you are building the habit you will always need in your professional life: the habit of reconsidering your own issues and expanding your self-awareness so that you may practice effectively.

Quadrant IV represents those issues that are unknown to self and unknown to others. This may be called the unconscious area. However, once the items in Quadrant II and Quadrant III are presented, Quadrant I is expanded and the issues in Quadrant IV are decreased.

MANAGING THE COUNTERTRANSFERENCE AND TRANSFERENCE (HEPWORTH, ROONEY, ROONEY, STROM-GOTTFRIED, & LARSON, 2010)

Countertransference occurs when the student has a reaction to the client's transference. Usually the transference may be a positive reaction to the worker's role. You may be seen as a good helper, a positive parenting figure. Or if you are setting limits on your client, you may be seen as a withholding figure. Students react unknowingly to clients' transference based on their own issues. In order to be helpful, one's own reactive countertransference has to be recognized, taken care of, and held at bay.

For example, imagine you are 24-year-old Ken, and you specifically requested not to be placed in substance abuse treatment. Your brother was an addict and the reactions you would have stemming from your own family issues would be too difficult and too painful to manage. Thus, you were given a second-year field placement in a mental health treatment program. This suited you well, and you believed that your family therapy experience and understanding of family dynamics would enhance your work with clients.

Your 26-year-old client came to understand the extent to which extended family was sabotaging her efforts to pursue a college education, and you helped her stay focused on her goals. Initially, your overidentification with her convinced you that she needed to pursue a four-year college degree as you had done. You learned in field instruction that her desire to enroll in a two-year hotel management program required your encouragement.

You also worked with a 55-year-old gay man who, up until recently, had been in the closet. This was foreign to you, as people now are able to be openly gay, and you expected him to be proud to accept himself. Your connection to him deepened as you came to understand the generational and political differences you had each encountered.

A client displays transference when he or she reacts to the social worker in the helping relationship in the same way he or she would have reacted to a parental authority. At times, a negative relationship may be exhibited. There may be anger about abandonment or an expectation of disappointment that represents a recreation of a historical relationship to an authority figure. As a social worker, one goal is to foster the client's positive transference in order to allow the work to proceed effectively. In the interaction, the worker will experience a reaction to the client's feelings and situations. This may result in a clarified understanding of the client's affects and needs. Or your countertransference may become a hindrance if your reactions are based on your unresolved issues.

For example, when the 40-year-old woman you were seeing revealed that her sister had been on crack and the family now had custody of her sister's children, your compassion led you to disclose that you had experienced a similar situation yourself. With your field instructor's help, you realized that your family issue is not relevant for discussion with the client. You were distracted by the parallels between your family's situation and the client's situation. While talking about your own story in field instruction, you concluded that by dwelling on comparisons you had omitted the children in the picture who needed parenting from your client. You realized the importance of strengthening the family's childrearing functions and saw that your countertransference had contributed to missing your client's need for help in the parenting role she and her mother shared. This understanding removed you from your own issue and prompted your reengagement with the client's issues.

Students all have their own issues. However, no matter the issue you'd like to avoid, it will surface sooner or later. Although you should protect yourself from overexposure to a painful issue, you can never be 100% avoidant. The student in the previous example can cope with an issue as it appeared with one client and gain strength through that situation that will carry over to other clients. However, if the majority of this student's clients were substance abusers, the countertransference would be overwhelming. If one of the student's clients had been the substance abuser, the student would likely have experienced a negative countertransference, especially if his or her own family situation was still an active one.

Do you defer going to social work school because you bring baggage? This answer depends upon whether you have resolved or are in the process of resolving your baggage issues. No one holds your baggage issues against you. These are the facts of living; these are your features, your attributes. If you have resolved many aspects of these issues, then certainly stay focused and productive in your social work school.

Ultimately, in your role as a student, you must be able to conduct yourself effectively and appropriately and provide help to others without being blocked by your own issues (Urdang, 2010).

USING YOUR HISTORY TO HELP OTHERS

Knowing your history does not mean disclosing it to clients. However, your self-awareness and insight will enrich your ability to work with clients. Therefore, you should embrace reflection and exploration of your own issues.

One student who is placed in a veterans program has firsthand knowledge of trauma and violence. Another student has firsthand knowledge of an eating disorder. Another student is in recovery for alcoholism. By the time these students have gotten to a social work program, at least some aspects of these issues should have been worked out or are currently being worked on. Continuous self-reflection will help them in their future role as social workers.

However, the practical question is raised about the extent to which this personal information should be shared in your initial interview at the agency, with your field instructor, with your school's field office, with your faculty field advisor, and with clients. These are multiple levels of self-disclosure.

The agency will have to know something about your history. This is the information in Quadrant I—the issues about you that are known to self and known to others. Your field instructor will have to be told along the way about Quadrant II—the issues that are known to self but unknown to others. This information will enhance your field instructor's understanding and enable a more individualized feedback that will expand Quadrant III—issues unknown to self but known to others.

The subtleties and nuances of your personal history will be used to help your work with clients. For example, your firsthand knowledge of eating disorders will have sensitized you to relevant issues that extend far beyond recognition of an eating disorder. Certain family dynamics will be familiar to you. You may be an athlete or a drama coach and through these perspectives you learned about public presentations.

Although very little is generally disclosed to clients, much of your personal history should be disclosed to your field instructor as it is relevant to your client work. In considering self-disclosures to clients, ask this question: Is this self-disclosure for their well-being? The use of self-disclosure must be viewed through the lens of practice theory, which comes from your readings and classroom teachings.

Beyond a student's family dynamics, supports, and disappointments, self-awareness should include the student's place in the social context of his or her schooling and social interactions. Understanding of the social institutional framework the student grew up in, the social networks he or she was engaged and not engaged with, the resources utilized by the family, and available and unavailable supports have utility.

One approach that can be used to highlight students' reflections about their relationships with people in their lives and social institutional resources in their communities utilizes several assessment factors identified by Hartman & Laird (1983). The assessment factors provided highlight ways of understanding relationships with family as well as environmental and community institutions. The following reflective exercise can be used to enhance your self-awareness.

REFLECTIVE EXERCISE

Phase 1. List the names of immediate family members, significant others, and friends in your household or life space. Label your relationship with each person in one of three ways—strong, conflicted, or distant.

Example: Joseph, brother—conflicted relationship; Johan, father—strong relationship; Stephanie, my lesbian significant other—strong relationship. The family does not know about her, or about my sexual orientation.

Phase 2. List relevant institutions in your community that may have significant bearing on your life. Label your relationship with these institutions in one of three ways—strong, conflicted, or distant.

Example: Notable University School of Social Work—strong relationship; field placement at family shelter—strong relationship; LGBT support group—strong relationship; parents' church—conflicted relationship; local hospital—distant relationship.

When students expand their awareness of their relationships with important persons in their lives they further their ability to recognize issues their clients may be having with important persons in their lives. In deepening their understanding of their own strong, conflicted, and distant interactions with community institutions students are better able to recognize strong, conflicted, and distant relationships their clients may have within their communities. This heightened self-awareness should accelerate students' use of skill in helping clients take stock of their personal connections and strengthen positive ties to vital community supports.

SUMMARY

Different types of self-awareness issues that impact students in the field experience have been identified. Six steps for attaining self-awareness in these domains have been provided in this chapter, which you should consider and utilize as you progress through your field experience. Your self-awareness will allow you to overcome issues that may inhibit your ability to practice effectively and improve your connection and work with clients.

Chapter 14 focuses on endings and transitions from school to employment and to licensing.

Chapter 14

Looking Toward the Future

INTRODUCTION

If you completed a bachelor in social work (BSW) or an master in social work (MSW) degree, you will undoubtedly have performed many acts that saved one life that in turn saved the entire world.

This chapter addresses the various issues related to ending field placement and moving on to the next field work year or to professional employment. These issues include taking stock of what you have learned; identifying and developing a path for future direction as a student; and embracing professional roles, including employment and licensure.

This chapter will help you gain perspective on the experiences of the foundation year of field work or second year of field work. Useful tools are provided to guide you as you reflect on the professional gains you have made.

ENDING FIRST-YEAR OR SENIOR-YEAR FIELD WORK

The fact that you have completed one major module or year of field work indicates that you have successfully navigated a portion of the path to becoming a competent social worker. You have learned to inform your actions by knowledge, values, self-reflection, and supervision.

A student reaching the end of a foundation BSW senior year or first year of field work and accompanying classes has demonstrated the ability to engage, assess, and intervene with clients using social work knowledge, values, and skills. The student has developed the reflective and research skills required to evaluate his or her work with clients and has shown attainment of the nine competencies of social work (Council on Social Work Education [CSWE], 2015).

Having concluded the foundation year, the student understands the social work role and what needs to be done with clients. The student is aware of his or her professional limitations and recognizes when to access supervision and agency help in order to assist clients.

A graduate with a BSW degree is able to work under supervision in many settings. These settings include mental health services, child welfare, community centers, nursing homes, or senior centers. He or she may work with high risk homeless families and children or in a school-based program.

TRANSITION FROM FIRST- TO SECOND-YEAR FIELD WORK

Upon the conclusion of first year, the student moving into second year will be required by the school to select an area of specialization. Field work and coursework will be determined by the specialization. The student should gather information from the school about their specializations' coursework and types of available field placements.

Picking a Specialization and Seeking Advice

The faculty at the school has designed specializations based on community needs, faculty expertise, and their assessment of the skills that graduates will require to find employment and contribute in high need areas. Maintain an open mind about the school's offerings rather than rigidly fixating on the concept that initially brought you to social work. Obtain feedback from your faculty field advisor and field instructor, and discuss with faculty coordinating the specializations regarding what you may learn in each. In selecting a specialization, think about your strengths and which of your talents you would like to develop more fully. Your school may offer specializations that you may never have heard of or considered upon starting in the program.

Repeating the Entry Process Into Second-Year Field Placement But With New Abilities

Whatever specialization the student selects, second-year field work builds on first year. Students will repeat the pattern of entry to their new setting and develop more skills needed to engage clients, make assessments, intervene effectively, and evaluate their work. The work will occur at a more sophisticated and deeper theoretical and practice level. Now, you will understand the process. Whether your specialization is community organization or clinical practice, upon completion you will be able to proceed as a social worker in any setting using your carefully developed professional skills.

TRANSITION FROM BSW TO CAREER OR TO MSW PROGRAM

The completion of college with a professional degree is not only an accomplishment but a life-altering experience to be cherished forever. After completing a BSW degree, the student may elect to find a job near the college, in his or her hometown, or some other unexplored location. Or the graduate may apply as an advanced standing student to a master in social work program. He or she may even decide to pursue alternate career paths often in related fields such as law or public administration or something entirely different.

Proceeding to an entry-level social work position or applying to an MSW program places the BSW graduate on a social work career path.

Applying for Employment

Graduates should take stock of the skills they have developed, identify further skills they may learn in a potential job, and find out the type of supervision being offered. Be open to the range of available employment opportunities. Entry-level openings may not necessarily be your dream job. However, the beginning position may be a place where staff are willing to teach you further. What a graduate will learn is more than can possibly be imagined.

One beginning BSW employee helped one family find housing and arrange the move to newer housing after a hurricane rendered their home uninhabitable. The new social worker's ability to provide for people after the unexpected crisis they faced furthered her understanding of her other clients who had crossed the border into her state as undocumented aliens. Another beginning employee had to ensure that the client in her guardianship program had a proper cremation. The new MSW employee met her ethical obligation by protecting the client's integrity after death, and as the representative of the agency entrusted with his guardianship, she scattered his ashes into the bay according to his wishes.

In evaluating a position, take into account the agency's level of professionalism, including the number of licensed social workers or staff. After completing the interview process, find out if a licensed social worker can supervise you. Asking the question at the start may preemptively close off a position with positive potential, but do not be hasty even though a licensed supervisor will support your future learning. An agency hiring a BSW graduate may be further professionalizing itself by hiring MSW graduates as well.

Prepare to present the field work you completed in your BSW program in a professional and thoughtful manner, showing the competencies that you have attained. Present a viable résumé, carefully scrutinized for content, spelling, and grammar. Keep it short. (See Appendix C template résumé for an example.) Prepare for job interviews by considering and reflecting upon the field work experiences you had with clients, the goals you had in working with them, and challenges you experienced in your role. Know in advance how you will discuss the way you handled the impact of clients' emotional issues. Finally, here is a reminder: *Never speak badly of your school, the faculty, your agency of field placement, or the field instruction you received.*

Applying to an MSW Program

If you decide to continue to an MSW program, you must prepare for the application process. Essays must be written that discuss your commitment to social work. Your application should present you and your accomplishments with honesty and candor. You will request letters of reference from the director of the BSW program and your faculty field advisor, and you must supply copies of your field evaluations. Schools may ask for several process recordings. In order to admit you with advanced standing status, MSW programs want to ensure that you have met all academic requirements including field work at the level of first year master's students. In addition, your grade point average (GPA) will have to meet standards for advanced standing students.

It is important to be forthcoming about anything in your past that would prevent you from being licensed in your state. Falsifying an application will make you ineligible for admission.

When proceeding to an MSW program, review and discuss the specialization selections at the programs where you are applying. Their field placement settings as well as coursework will support the second year specializations. Consider these areas and include your interest in your application.

TRANSITION FROM MSW TO CAREER

At last, you have graduated from your social work program with an MSW. You completed a demanding experience, and you should be proud. Reflect upon who you were before beginning your social work education; you will see that you have undergone a huge transformation.

Licensing Exam Preparation

Now you will have to pass the state licensing exam. Take the preparatory classes, and do your best to make the financial investment in obtaining the best and most intensive training available. Some of your schools will offer training. If your training does not consist of an intensive two-day program, it will only be a start. Purchase the preparatory books with the relevant content areas presented in outline form. Read through each section carefully. *Do not skim the material.* This is a habit you must get into if you are to pass the exam. *Read. Every. Single. Word. Completely.* This will prepare you for test taking. All questions must be read completely to locate the key words in the question. At the end of each section, you will find quizzes. Take the quiz under quiet conditions. After you have read through the material, then grade it. Do not waste the questions by taking them before a thorough review of the content. You are taking the practice quizzes to see how much you know and if you understand each type of exam question.

Most social work students are not adept at taking short-answer exams. They know how to write essays and papers and create presentations. The test-taking courses provide you with techniques and approaches to bolster your confidence in taking this type of test. You have to know the content areas.

Résumé Preparation

At the same time that you begin reviewing for the licensing exam, you will undoubtedly want to prepare for locating employment. First, write a résumé. (See Figure 14.1 and Appendix C for sample résumés.) Please, nothing overdone. You are trying to obtain a job as a professional whose credentials stand for themselves. Do not solicit advice from people who are not social workers. The résumé should be suitable for your profession, not for someone else's. Including pictures of yourself is not appropriate. Lengthy statements about your objectives should be omitted. Employers want to know what you did, what skills you have, what credentials you have earned, your field placements, and prior employment. Keep it brief and accurate.

Once your résumé is complete, write cover letters and e-mails to send to future employers. While the résumé may be suitable for almost any job you may be applying for, your cover letter should be individually prepared for the position you are seeking, highlighting your background to match the available job.

Employment Reference From School

When a student graduates with an MSW degree, the faculty field advisor typically has the task of writing the student's employment reference. It is kept on file by the school and upon the student's request, it is sent to future employers. This document highlights the student's growth, strengths and accomplishments in the program, and shows future learning needs. The student's field placements are described, and the significant aspects of the learning experiences in first-year and second-year settings are put forth. Usually the student signs off on the employment reference before it may be sent out. The graduate may request the school to forward letters of reference to any position where he or she has applied.

Figure 14.1   Sample Professional Résumé

RÉSUMÉ

Moose Elliott
95 Gold Rush Alley
Rocky Mountain, Alaska
(444) 790-xxxx moose40.elliott@e-mail.com

EDUCATION

Alaska School of Social Work   Master in Social Work May 2016
Rain Forest, Alaska

Massachusetts School of Oceanography   Bachelor of Arts 2014
Major: Marine Biology, Magna Cum Laude

FIELD PLACEMENTS

Second Year – Specialization in Clinical Social Work   September 2015–May 2016
Community, Family and Mental Health Center
A multiservice program for the community
Rain Forest, Alaska

- Conducted Individual and group counseling with clients with behavioral health disorders
  - Developed diagnostic skills using *DSM–5*
  - Utilized clinical interventions to sustain and support vulnerable clients
- Consulted remotely with team psychiatrist and other professionals
- Transferred crisis cases to psychiatric facility by air to Anchorage
- Group work with teens focused on socialization, postsecondary school goals
  - Dealt with issues of sexuality, family, and interpersonal conflict
- Received individual supervision from licensed social worker weekly
- Prepared and submitted weekly process recordings for supervisory review

First Year – Generic Social Work   September 2014–May 2015
Department of Social Services
Homer, Alaska

- Provided counseling for mothers of children at risk of neglect and abuse. Populations were primarily single parents whose incomes had been significantly reduced due to economic downturn in fishing.
- Co-led group with educator to teach parenting skills
- Located and assessed potential foster home setting in the event these were needed for children with seriously ill parents
- Developed peer helpers for parents in need comprised of senior citizen volunteers
- Matched peer helpers to families for child care and respite help

EMPLOYMENT

Oil Rig – Exxon   July 2002–August 2010
Off shore
And Pipeline oversight
Alaska and Canada

VOLUNTEER EXPERIENCE   Summers 2009–present

Coach to Apprentice Training Program

- Teacher/mentor in apprentice training program to develop skills for working in an oil rig

Although future employers should know that they do not have the right to ask for your field work evaluation, sometimes they do. This is a confidential educational document between you, the agency field educators, and the school. If you are asked for such a document, do not produce it. You should contact the school's field office for direction.

Utilizing Your Networks

All networks that students have developed while in the program should be utilized. Your efforts to be seen as a student who does more than what is asked, is timely, and works diligently on behalf of clients show you to be collegial and trustworthy. This will present you in a favorable light when you are seeking employment. Agency staff may give you leads—they may know about a job at a friend's agency. In addition, visit agency websites and locate their human resources departments. Discover your university's career department office.

It pays to attend meetings at your school to learn about other settings. Write down names, keep business cards, and organize a file of every speaker you have heard at school and out of school. Attending any event you are invited to boosts your morale and puts you in circulation. Avoid the "Eh, it doesn't mean much" attitude. It does mean something—sometimes it means a job opportunity. When you are looking for employment, reach out through e-mail or by mail. Other professionals will value the fact that you took note of them and kept track of their program. They will appreciate your proactivity.

CASE ILLUSTRATION 14.1

STUDENT USING NETWORKS TO FIND JOB OPPORTUNITIES

Orin has completed a second-year placement in a substance abuse treatment program in a unique methadone maintenance (MM) program that conducted group and individual treatment. He had a very successful year at the program, throwing himself into the groups—an activity he never thought he would like.

He would like to continue working in substance abuse treatment. Most of the clients have been African American and Latino, and he, being a "nice Irish boy," thought it would be hard for him to be accepted. He received encouragement from his field instructor and the clients seemed to take an instant liking to him. In fact,

(Continued)

(Continued)

he later found out in their discussions that they enjoyed that he was different from them, and he learned much from them about their dilemmas as well as their various cultures.

One friend at school told him that her agency was hiring, and since she was leaving, she wanted Orin to apply. She offered to bring his résumé to the program director and promised to share his strengths and virtues. At the same time, Orin's field instructor volunteered several names of colleagues in other substance treatment agencies and he has written to them. One site is a residential program for adolescents in foster care, most of whom are minority kids. Orin's positive experience at this agency has given him confidence in his skills, and he feels equipped and ready to handle this job. He prepared a résumé, and his e-mail was well written:

Dear Ms. Lawrence,

I am about to graduate from Flintstone School of Social Work with an MSW degree. My field instructor, Ms. Sasha Tallmadge, provided your information and suggested I write to you in the event there might be a position available at Wonder Kids Program. Attached is my résumé. My degree will be awarded in two weeks, at which time I will be able to take the licensing exam.

This past year I have learned to do group work and provide individual therapy. Many of the clients I worked with were late adolescents and quite diverse. Through field instruction, I have been challenged to develop my skills, especially in terms of understanding latent content and developing self-awareness. Working with youth in your program is an assignment I am very enthusiastic to undertake. If there is an available position, I hope you will be able to provide me with an opportunity to meet with you.

Thank you for your consideration. I look forward to hearing from you.

Sincerely,
Orin Burton
OBurton@e-mail.com
917-555-xxxx

Discussion

Orin is using his network well, and his contacts are willing to give him leads at the end of his field work enterprise. It is best to embrace every possibility you find. Write to each person, and apply for positions even if you feel the commute is too long or the salary is too low. Sometimes surprises are waiting.

CASE ILLUSTRATION 14.2

STUDENT WITH CONFLICTUAL RELATIONSHIP WITH TRAINING DIRECTOR

Pamela had some difficulty at her agency because the placement was not well organized when she began. Most of the students were not assigned to their sites right away, and Pamela had to wait three weeks before her site in the clinic was ready. The training program was too long—most likely to compensate for the late start. She felt taken advantage of and made it clear at the beginning to the training director, and after to her field instructor, that she was frustrated. Now that she is looking for a job, she has become more reflective about the fact that she alienated the training director. She has learned the importance of being less reactive and more contained. But as far as this situation is concerned, she believes it is too late.

Her relationship with the agency has been somewhat conflicted because she had a hard time letting go of her negative feelings about the late start, having held on to her anger up until now. She kept working at the site because of her clients. She would actually like a job at this setting but is pessimistic about that. Her field instructor has been supportive of her and commends her work and growth. Because of her positive relationship with clients, she is hoping to sidestep the training director, who, luckily for Pamela, has gone on maternity leave for three months.

Pamela decides to ask her faculty field advisor's opinion about what strategy she can use. The advisor suggests that she speak to her field instructor. She concurs that for Pamela's sake it is a good thing the training director is on leave. Pamela took her advice and had a conversation with her field instructor regarding positions, asking to discuss possible agencies where she might apply for a job.

Discussion

Pamela is learning how to be strategic and through the process of considering how to secure employment she has come to understand her particular limitations better, especially that she is easily reactive. Reflecting on the way she handled the late start caused her to realize that she may have damaged her reputation, which has been positive for her. She utilized interpersonal skills effectively and showed that she has the self-correcting mechanisms to recover from an unfavorable situation. She is a graduate who is on the right path for professional development. Pamela had been feeling blocked, but after speaking with her advisor she had a better plan in mind.

SUMMARY

This chapter has presented you with various ways in which you may consider your forward movement whether you have completed a BSW degree or an MSW degree. It has offered several concrete approaches for utilizing networks, focusing on licensure, and obtaining employment. If you have completed a year of field work and plan to continue to the next year, rereading this text before you begin the new year should be very helpful to you.

Everyone associated with this book wishes you great success as you move forward in this generous and humanitarian profession.

Epilogue

> Whoever preserves a single life is considered
> by Scripture as if he preserved an entire world.
>
> —*Mishnah Sanhedrin 4:5*

So many situations presented in this volume are representative of students' dilemmas, and all of their "perfect imperfections" (Legend & Gad, 2013). What has to be grasped upon completing a social work program with a bachelor in social work (BSW) or with a master in social work (MSW) is that everything is a perfect imperfection. Relationships are messy, and throughout, relationships require communication; reflection; and, most of all, commitment to the relationship. This holds true in relationships with clients, field instructors, faculty, and other students.

To sustain the generosity and humanitarianism to preserve a single life, hold on to your wherewithal to reflect and to further your personal and professional growth—step by step.

Notes and References

CHAPTER 1: INTRODUCTION TO FIELD WORK: EXPERIENTIAL EDUCATION

Bogo, M., & Vayda, E. J. (1998). *The practice of field instruction in social work: Theory and process* (2nd ed.). New York, NY: Columbia University Press.

Dewey, J. (1963). *Experience and education*. New York, NY: Collier Books. (Original work published 1938)

Gardner, H., & Shulman, L. S. (2005). The professions in America today: Crucial but fragile. *Daedalus, 134*(3), 13–18.

Goldstein, H. (1993). Field education for reflective practice: A re-constructive proposal. *Journal of Teaching in Social Work, 8*(1, 2), 165–182.

Honey, P., & Mumford, A. (2006). *The learning styles questionnaire, 80-item version*. Maidenhead, UK: Peter Honey Publications.

Kolb, D. A. (1984). *Experiential learning: Experience as the source of learning and development* (Vol. 1). Englewood Cliffs, NJ: Prentice-Hall.

Luft, J., & Ingham, H. (1955). The Johari window, a graphic model of interpersonal awareness. *Proceedings of the Western training laboratory in group development*. Los Angeles, CA: UCLA.

Reynolds, B. (1948). *Learning and teaching in the practice of social work*. New York, NY: Farrar and Rinehart.

Schon, D. (1984). *The reflective practitioner*. New York, NY: Basic Books.

Schon, D. (1990). *Educating the reflective practitioner.* New York, NY: Wiley.

Shulman, L. S. (2005). Signature pedagogies in the professions. *Daedalus, 134*(3), 52–59.

Notes:

Delphi (7th century BCE). The inscription "Gnothi seauton" is found on the Temple of Apollo at Delphi. It was further popularized by Socrates.

In *Experiential Learning: Experience as the Source of Learning and Development* (Vol. 1), Kolb cites four types of learners:

1. Diverging Learning Style Concrete Experience/Reflective Observation (CE/RO): The learner who is focused on concrete experience and reflective observation
2. Assimilating Learning Style Abstract Conceptualization/Reflective Observation (AC/RO): The learner tending to favor linking abstract concepts with reflective observation
3. Converging Learning Style Abstract Conceptualization/Active Experimentation (AC/AE): The learner using abstract conceptualization to create action.
4. Accommodating Concrete Experience/Active Experimentation (CE/AE): The learner using experience to guide the development of future action.

Chapter 2: The Social Work Professional Role in Field Work

Council on Social Work Education. (2015). *Educational policy and accreditation standards.* Alexandria, VA: Author.

Chapter 3: Getting Accepted By the Agency

American Psychiatric Association. (2000). *Diagnostic and statistical manual of mental disorders* (4th ed., text rev.). Washington, DC: Author.

American Psychiatric Association. (2013). *Diagnostic and statistical manual of mental disorders* (5th ed.). Washington, DC: Author.

Emeril Lagasse. (2015). Biography.com. Retrieved from http://www/biography.com/people/emeril-lagasse-9542380

Work Ethic. (2015). In *Merriam-Webster Collegiate Dictionary.* Retrieved from http://unabridged.merriam-webster.com/collegiate/work%20ethic

Chapter 4: Developing Social Work Competencies

Council on Social Work Education. (2015). *Educational policy and accreditation standards.* Alexandria, VA: Author.

Gardner, H., & Shulman, L. S. (2005). The professions in America today: Crucial but fragile. *Daedalus, 134*(3), 13–18.

National Association of Social Workers. (2008). *Code of ethics.* Washington, DC: NASW Press.

NYU Silver School of Social Work. (2015). *Field learning evaluation: Advanced concentration (second year).* Retrieved from http://socialwork.nyu.edu/content/dam/sssw/academics/msw/pdf/Advanced%20Concentration%20Mid-Year%20%26%20Final%20Evaluation.pdf

Shulman, L. S. (2005). Signature pedagogies in the professions. *Daedalus, 134*(3), 52–59.

Wurzweiler School of Social Work, Yeshiva University. (2014). *Field instruction manual* (pp. 34, 37, 42, 43, 51, 52). Retrieved from http://www.yu.edu/uploadedFiles/Academics/Graduate/Wurzweiler%20School%20of%20Social%20Work/Fieldwork/FIELD%20MANUAL%20REVISED%20FEB2013.pdf

Chapter 5: Field Instructor as Coach

Bogo, M., & Vayda, E. J. (1998). *The practice of field instruction in social work: theory and process* (2nd ed.). New York, NY: Columbia University Press.

Luft, J., & Ingham, H. (1955). The Johari window, a graphic model of interpersonal awareness. *Proceedings of the Western training laboratory in group development.* Los Angeles, CA: UCLA.

Reynolds, B. (1942). *Learning and teaching in the practice of social work.* New York, NY: Farrar and Rhinehart.

Schon, D. (1990). *Educating the reflective practitioner.* New York, NY: Wiley.

Chapter 6: Process Recording—The Primary Educational Tool

American Psychiatric Association. (2013). *Diagnostic and statistical manual of mental disorders* (5th ed.). Washington, DC: Author.

New York State. (2014, July). *NYS OMH single point of access (SPOA) care coordination/ACT Program application.* Retrieved from http://www.nyc.gov/html/doh/downloads/pdf/mental/spoa-urf.pdf

New York State. (n.d.). *Global assessment of functioning.* Retrieved from https://www.omh.ny.gov/omhweb/childservice/mrt/global_assessment_functioning.pdf

Shulman, L. (2011). *The skills of helping individuals, families, groups and communities* (7th ed.). New York, NY: Cengage Learning.

Chapter 7: The Relationship Between Faculty Field Advisor and Student

National Association of Social Workers. (2008). *Code of ethics.* Washington, DC: NASW Press.

Chapter 8: Timelines for Student Development

American Psychiatric Association. (2013). *Diagnostic and statistical manual of mental disorders* (5th ed.). Washington, DC: Author.

Reynolds, B. (1942). *Learning and teaching in the practice of social work.* New York, NY: Farrar and Rhinehart.

Shulman, L. (2011). *The skills of helping individuals, families, groups and communities* (7th ed.). New York, NY: Cengage Learning.

Note:

Delphi (7th century BCE). The inscription "Gnothi seauton" is found on the Temple of Apollo at Delphi. It was further popularized by Socrates.

Chapter 9: Developing Social Work Competencies in the Foundation Year

Council on Social Work Education. (2015). *Educational policy and accreditation standards.* Alexandria, VA: Author.

Glassman, U. (2008). *Group work: A humanistic and skills building approach* (2nd ed.). Thousand Oaks, CA: Sage.

National Association of Social Workers. (2008). *Code of ethics.* Washington, DC: NASW Press.

Shulman, L. (2015). *Skills of helping individuals, families, groups and communities* (8th ed.). Independence, KY: Cengage Learning.

Chapter 10: Advanced Competencies in the Second Year

Council on Social Work Education. (2015). *Educational policy and accreditation standards.* Alexandria, VA: Author.

National Association of Social Workers. (2008). *Code of ethics.* Washington, DC: NASW Press.

Simmons College School of Social Work. (2015). *Field education manual* (p. 4). Retrieved from http://internal.simmons.edu/students/ssw/msw-students/field-education/field-education-manual

Chapter 12: Managing Stressful Relationships and Demands

Burnet, J. (1892). *Early Greek philosophy.* Herakleitos of Ephesos (535 BCE to 474 BCE) (p. 136). London and Edinburgh: Adam and Charles Black.

Shulman, L. (2006). The clinical supervisor–practitioner working alliance: A parallel process. *The Clinical Supervisor, 24*(1/2), 23–47.

Williams, A. (1997). On parallel process in social work supervision. *Clinical Social Work Journal, 25*(4), 425–435.

Chapter 13: Utilizing Self-Awareness in Social Work Practice

Hepworth, D. H., Rooney, R. H., Rooney, D. G., Strom-Gottfried, K., & Larson, J. (2010). *Direct social work practice—Theory and skills* (8th ed.). Belmont, CA: Brooks/Cole.

Luft, J., & Ingham, H. (1955). The Johari window, a graphic model of interpersonal awareness. *Proceedings of the Western training laboratory in group development.* Los Angeles, CA: UCLA.

Hartman, A., & Laird, J. (1983). *Family centered social work practice.* New York, NY: Free Press.

Urdang, E. (2010). Awareness of self—A critical tool. *Social Work Education, 29*(5), 523–538.

Chapter 14: Looking Toward the Future

Council on Social Work Education. (2015). *Educational policy and accreditation standards.* Alexandria, VA: Author.

Epilogue

Legend, J., & Gad, T. (Writers). (2013). All of me. On *Love in the Future* [CD]. Los Angeles, CA: Columbia.

Appendix A

Process Recording Outlines

Process Recording

Narrative Format

Part I Pre-Engagement

Student's preparation includes what information you gleaned about the client's situation and circumstances, and preparatory empathy—your ability to put yourself in the client's shoes.

Part II Narrative: Tell the story of interaction with client(s).

The longest portion of several pages includes description, observation, dialogue, and summary of session themes.

Part III Impressions

Describe reactions to the session. How do you feel it went? What highlights were important?

Part IV Plans for Future Action

Part V   Questions for Field Instructor

Process Recording
Column Format

Part I Pre-Engagement: Describe your cognitive preparation for the meeting and your preparatory empathy.

_____

_____

_____

_____

_____

_____

_____

Part II Client Session (longest section—continues for several pages)

<u>Dialogue</u>   <u>Student's Feelings</u>   <u>Your Intentions</u>   <u>Relevant Theory</u>   <u>Field Instructor Comments</u>

Part III Impressions

Part IV Plans for Future Action

Part V Questions for Field Instructor

Process Recording
Format for Group Work

Name of Group:

Session Number: Meeting Date:

Group Members Present: Give every member a disguised name, and maintain these
                        throughout.

Group Members Absent: Disguise the names.

Pre-Engagement

Include issues from prior sessions and your preparation for addressing these.

Narrative

Use quotes, summarize interaction, and give each member a disguised name.

In summarizing, identify session themes. Clearly present your interventions. Include your observations and understanding of group dynamics, participation and communication patterns, and group norms.

Describe any activities of the group and the interactions that occurred.

(Longest section)

Impressions

Briefly share your reactions to the meeting.

Plans for Future Action

Questions for Field Instructor

Appendix B

Field Placement Planning Form

Second Year

Please complete this three-page form in order to begin the placement process for second year of field work. This form will be used to plan your field placement experience and will be sent to your field placement agency.

Mr. _____ Ms. _____

Name _____   Date _____

      (Last)   (First)

Student ID # _____   Home Phone _____

Present Address _____   Office Phone _____

_____   E-Mail _____

Summer Address   Cell Phone _____

_____

_____

      (City)   (State/Zip)

Fall Address (If different from present address)

_____

Do you speak a language other than English? _____   Specify _____

MSW DEGREE PROGRAM

Check off all that apply:

Field Placement at Place of Employment (   )

School-Assigned Field Placement (   )

CONCENTRATION _____

FIRST-YEAR FIELD PLACEMENT DESCRIPTION

Agency Name _____

Type of Agency _____

Student Assignments (List):

Client Population:

Practice Methods/Modalities Used:

WORK EXPERIENCE IN SOCIAL WORK AND OTHER FIELDS

Please provide information on the last two jobs you have had, starting with the most recent one.

Dates	Agency or Firm	Position and Duties

VOLUNTEER ACTIVITIES (welfare, educational, civic, political, etc.):

Dates	Agency or Firm	Position and Duties

REQUESTED OPPORTUNITIES FOR SECOND-YEAR FIELD PLACEMENT

Please indicate a range of **special interests** you have. If you are employed and will be doing your field placement at your job, take into account the available opportunities that your agency can offer.

Type of Populations:

Practice Methods (individual work, family, groups, and community social work):

Other Learning Opportunities:

STUDENT'S LEARNING GOALS FOR SECOND YEAR

- Identify some professional roles and skills you wish to develop. Discuss their relevancy to your chosen concentration.
- Describe the types of assignments that should help you meet these goals.

Special Factors:

Please list any factors/circumstances that should be taken into consideration when planning your field placement: geography, time, physical condition, religious observance, family commitments, etc.:

Are you dependent on public transportation? Yes _____   No _____

Driver's License: Yes _____   No _____   Availability of Car: Yes _____   No _____

Appendix C

Sample Résumé

Quiche Lorraine
1422 Boulevard St. Michele
Paris, France
(342) 290-xxxx   quiche.lorraine@xxx.fr

EDUCATION

Paris School of Social Work   Master in Social Work May 2016
Paris, France

London School of Economics   Bachelor of Arts 2012
Major: Philosophy, Magna Cum Laude

FIELD PLACEMENTS

Second Year – Specialization in Clinical Social Work September 2015–May 2016
Institute for Psychosocial Therapy
Lyon, France

- Individual counseling of clients with schizophrenia, bipolar disorder, and other diagnoses
- Group work in day treatment program—conducted activities therapy group, creative writing group, and women's group with patients in day treatment program
- Crisis Mobile Unit—ACT team member
    Conducted outreach and crisis intervention with team to provide medication for patients, monitor their well-being, and prevent rehospitalization
- Received individual supervision from licensed social worker weekly
- Prepared and submitted weekly process recordings for supervisory review

First Year – Generic Social Work   September 2014–May 2015
Odeon Community Center
453 Boulevard St. Germaine
Paris, France

- Worked with immigrant mothers of children in early intervention program. Populations were primarily from African and Middle Eastern countries. Met weekly in group. Saw individual mothers.
- Focus on children's French language development skills to prepare them for school
- Worked with education staff in teaching parenting skills and child development for mothers
- Facilitated adolescent group of girls to focus on issues related to school, culture conflict with parents, and friendship and other relationships

EMPLOYMENT

French Language Teacher   September 2012–May 2014
Manchester High School
Manchester, UK

- Teach beginning and advanced French classes to ethnically diverse high school students
- Create innovative program inviting native French speakers to classroom
- Develop anti-bullying program and curriculum for the school

Camp Counselor and Unit Head   Summers 2009–2012
Orchard Street YMCA Settlement Camp
New York, NY, USA

- Theater director for French language production

VOLUNTEER EXPERIENCE   September 2010–2012

Intergeneration Projects
Seniors and high school students
Manchester, UK

Index

Note: In page references, f indicates figures.